# ALDO LEOPOLD

## A Fierce Green Fire

by Marybeth Lorbiecki

OXFORD UNIVERSITY PRESS
NEW YORK OXFORD

Oxford University Press

Oxford New York
Athens Auckland Bangkok Bogotá Buenos Aires Calcutta
Cape Town Chennai Dar es Salaam Delhi Florence Hong Kong Istanbul
Karachi Kuala Lumpur Madrid Melbourne Mexico City Mumbai
Nairobi Paris São Paulo Singapore Taipei Tokyo Toronto Warsaw

*and associated companies in*

Berlin Ibadan



First published in 1996 by Falcon Publishing Co., Inc.
Helena and Billings, Montana

First issued as an Oxford University Press paperback, 1999



Library of Congress Cataloging-in-Publication Data
Lorbiecki, Marybeth.
Aldo Leopold : a fierce green fire / Marybeth Lorbiecki.
p. cm.
Originally published: Helena, Mont. : Falcon Press, © 1996.
Includes bibliographical references and index.
ISBN 0-19-512966-0 (pbk.)
1. Leopold, Aldo, 1886-1948. 2. Naturalists--Wisconsin--Biography. 3. Conservationists--Wisconsin--Biography. Title.
QH31.L618L68 1999
333.7'2'092--dc21
[B] 98-52349

10 9 8 7 6 5 4 3 2 1

Printed in the United States of America

*For my David*

# Acknowledgments

With special thanks to Nina Leopold Bradley, for sharing her loving memories of her father and giving me access to family papers and photographs; to Curt Meine, without whose research and compelling writing this project could not and would not have been attempted. Additional gratitude to my editor, Megan Hiller; Bernie Schermetzler of the University of Wisconsin Archives; Charles Luthin of The Aldo Leopold Foundation; the late Robert A. McCabe, Richard McCabe, Kevin McCabe, and Marie McCabe; Betty Beck and Helen Parsons of the Des Moines County Historical Society; Steven Brower; Cheryl of the Forest Historical Society; Robert Torres of the New Mexico Commission of Public Records; Mrs. Albert (Joan) Hochbaum; Peter and Joyce Ward of the Delta Duck Station; Marilyn Love of Lawrenceville School; Carolyn Leopold Michaels and Dr. Bruce Carl Leopold; Michael Quinn, Museum Photographer at the Grand Canyon National Park; Carol Severance of Grey Towers National Historic Landmark; Russ Sewell of Pheasants Forever; Ron Young of the National Agricultural Library; William R. Jordan III of the University of Wisconsin-Madison Arboretum; Gary Laib; Gaylord Nelson, Robert Eberhart, and Patricia Byrnes of The Wilderness Society; Dr. Julie Dunlap, Mary Beth Nierengarten, Ann Clark, and Jill Anderson.

Also thanks to John Lorbiecki, Paul Rome, Myrna and Chuck Olsen, and Darryl Mataya, who generously provided technological assistance; and of course, to my husband and canoe partner, David, for always and everything.

*There are some who can live without wild things*
*and some who cannot.*
*These essays are the delights and dilemmas*
*of one who cannot.*

*Foreword to* A Sand County Almanac

# Contents


| | |
|---|---|
| Author's Note | ix |
| Introduction | xi |
| Lug-ins-land: 1887-1901 | 1 |
| Ornithologists and Explorations: 1901-1903 | 15 |
| The Naturalist Out East: 1903-1905 | 21 |
| Women and Wise Use: 1905-1909 | 31 |
| A Cowboy in Love: 1909-1912 | 39 |
| New Life and Near Death: 1912-1914 | 53 |
| Save that Game: 1915-1919 | 65 |
| A Wild Proposal: 1919-1924 | 83 |
| Surveying the Field: 1924-1933 | 97 |
| The Land Laboratories: 1933-1936 | 123 |
| The Professor: 1937-1939 | 145 |
| Paths of Violence: 1939-1945 | 157 |
| Great Possessions: 1945-1948 | 171 |
| Afterword | 181 |
| A Daughter's Reflections by Nina Leopold Bradley | 185 |
| Notes | 189 |
| Books by Aldo Leopold | 203 |
| Selected References | 204 |
| Index | 207 |

# Author's Note

*We shall never achieve harmony with the land,*
*any more than we shall achieve*
*absolute justice or liberty for people.*
*In these higher aspirations the important thing*
*is not to achieve but to strive.*

*"Natural History,"* A Sand County Almanac

After a long day of rain, wind, and swampy portages, we pitch our tent. A misty blanket settles over the melon-tinted horizon, and the long, eerie trilling of a loon drifts over the water.

Neither humming motors nor exhaust dull our spirits. City lights do not dim the skies. The stars are crisp and startling in the blackness, and the air smells of pine. Later, if we are lucky, the distant howl of a wolf will jerk us out of sleep.

No directions came with this country. The island could have become the site of a tourist condominium or a shopping mall for boaters. But in the 1930s and 40s, Aldo Leopold and other lovers of the outdoors saw the lakes between Minnesota and Ontario for what they were—places of rugged beauty and unspoiled nature that, once lost, could never be recovered. They called for a halt to unthinking "progress," for a chance to rest in what was and is, and to preserve something for the future.

Aldo Leopold helped put the wilderness debate on the national agenda, and for this, I am grateful. His writings and his life have inspired and enriched me, but it is the lands he helped preserve that nourish me most.

most. Because of this, I continually return to him, so that I, too, might learn how to live on the land and pass it on in healthier shape than I encountered it.

# INTRODUCTION

*Like winds and sunsets, wild things were taken for granted*
*until progress began to do away with them.*
*Now we face the question whether a still higher 'standard of living'*
*is worth its cost in things natural, wild, and free.*
*For us of the minority, the opportunity to see geese*
*is more important than television,*
*and the chance to find a pasque-flower*
*is a right as inalienable as free speech.*

*Foreword to* A Sand County Almanac

For those of us who have often read *A Sand County Almanac*, these words are as familiar and beloved as our backpacks, canoes, and walking sticks. They evoke that other world in which we shake off the burdens of overstuffed calendars, eye-straining computers, bleeping answering machines, dull textbooks, and traffic. The words urge us to rethink who we are and how we are living.

For those who have not read the *Almanac,* nor heard of Aldo Leopold, his words may sound like those of a contemporary environmentalist. They should. Though Leopold died in 1948, his writings, research, and teaching have formed the framework of discussions about land use for more than half a decade.

Leopold is internationally recognized as the father of modern wildlife management and ecology and the chair of the field's first university department. His textbook, *Game Management*, was the definitive text for decades; it has been recently reprinted. As for *A Sand County Almanac,* Leopold's book of personal essays, it has sold over a million copies and has been translated into German, French, Russian, Japanese, and Chinese. It has been dubbed "the environmentalists' bible," and Leopold has been hailed as an American prophet.

Leopold's influence, however, goes far beyond the *Almanac* and *Game Management*. More than five hundred of his essays, articles, handbooks, reviews, and newsletters were published in his lifetime, and nearly as many remain unpublished or are currently under consideration for publication (not including his letters and journals). He was a member of more than a hundred clubs and societies, many of which continue to follow the course Leopold set. The first wilderness area in a national forest, and thus the beginning of our wilderness system, was also the work of Leopold.

It's hard to say what the American landscape might look like if Aldo Leopold hadn't come along when he did. His discoveries and policy recommendations drove forward the emerging fields of forestry, soil conservation, wildlife study and management, ecology, wilderness protection, land restoration, and environmental ethics.

Yet how many Americans have even heard of Leopold?

Relatively few. Perhaps he was involved in too many aspects of the conservation movement to be pigeonholed into an easily remembered historical slot. Perhaps he has not joined Thoreau in American folk history because his writings challenge cultural rather than just individual assumptions: he wrote that "to change ideas about what land is for is to change ideas about what anything is for."[1]

Whatever the reason, the majority of Americans have not yet been introduced to this person who has been so influential in their lives. Even many *Almanac* devotees know little about how Leopold's thinking evolved, or about his life. This is a shame; it is a life well worth knowing.

Leopold wasn't born inspired, and he didn't achieve a long string of school degrees. He followed his curiosity, made mistakes, and ate his words more than once. He summed up for many the questions, the conflicts, and the longings of an ecological approach to life.

Aldo Leopold's greatest dream was to learn how to live on the land without spoiling it. In his life and writings, he came closer than most of us will ever come. That is, unless we too let the land settle into our bones.

# Lug-ins-land
## 1887-1901

*When I call to mind my earliest impressions,*
*I wonder whether the process ordinarily referred to as growing up*
*is not actually a process of growing down. . . .*
*my earliest impressions of wildlife and its pursuit*
*retain a vivid sharpness of form, color, and atmosphere*
*that half a century of professional wildlife experience*
*has failed to obliterate or improve upon.*

*"Red Legs Kicking,"* A Sand County Almanac

From his childhood home atop Prospect Hill in Burlington, Iowa, Aldo Leopold could gaze out over the mighty Mississippi and its wet, wooded bottomlands. Each fall and spring, the skies were speckled like the breast of a wood thrush as thousands of migrating birds flew overhead, rousing hunters to their blinds. Coal smoke wafted up from the river's steamboats. The train whistles of the Chicago, Burlington & Quincy Railroad pierced the winds as locomotives chugged back and forth across the Burlington bridge, linking Illinois to Iowa.

Though unaware of it, Leopold was overlooking the meeting of the nation's East and West, of the industrial revolution and the frontier, of an age of nature's plenty and one of scarcity, of the nineteenth century and the twentieth to come.

Leopold was born in Burlington on January 11, 1887, in the house of his grandparents, Charles and Marie Runge Starker. Their home provided fertile soil for the growth of a citizen concerned about people, the land,

and the relationships between them. As some flowers are colored by minerals absorbed in their roots, Aldo's later works exhibit shades of his grandparents and parents.

Des Moines County Historical Society

*A view of Burlington, Iowa, from Prospect Hill.*

A German immigrant educated in engineering and architecture, Charles Starker had come to Burlington in 1850, when it was a rough river town on the edge of the western prairie. He liked what he saw, because it reminded him of his homeland, and he worked to make Burlington even more into the kind of town he wanted it to be: aesthetic, prosperous, and cultured. Over the years, he progressed from the drafting of buildings to the construction of businesses, excelling as a grocer, banker, alderman, and director of the city cemetery. Using his prestige, he spearheaded efforts to bring to the town, among other civic gems, a library and an opera house, which lent Burlington a grand style scarcely matched by other Midwestern communities its size.[1] But style was not enough.

Charles was an amateur naturalist, and he believed that cities, as well as homes, required spaces specifically set aside for people to enjoy nature's offerings. He convinced city leaders to look to the future: though

Burlington was surrounded by woods and prairies, they needed to buy up land on the outskirts of town for a large park. Charles designed the park to flow along the natural contours of the land, enhanced by native plants rather than with the formal, European-style ornamentals common in gardens of the time. The park, known as Crapo Park, wrapped around a lake that was eventually named for Charles—Starker Lake.

Steven Brower

*Aldo's grandparents, Charles and Marie Runge Starker, about 1895.*

Charles and Marie Starker had moved from Burlington's North Hill neighborhood to the Prospect Hill bluff in the 1870s, when their daughter Clara (Aldo's mother) was still a teenager.[2] They bought an ornate Italianate mansion, with gingerbread trim and a grand, two-story bay window facing the Mississippi. The Starkers filled the high-ceilinged rooms with books, mirrors, polished wooden furniture, richly flowered fabrics, and the music of Clara's piano. But the land surrounding their new home was not as easily enhanced. It had been cut up during the construction of the house and left scoured by the wind. Formal gardens had gone untended. Wild grapevines and blackberry brambles had taken over the yard, and water snakes slid through the thorny underbrush.

Yet Charles saw promise in the ruined acres. He enlisted Marie and the two children, Arthur and Clara, to help him transform the limestone plateau into a proper yard and garden. Together they thrust all kinds of plants into the rocky dirt and kept them watered: pines, spruces, oaks, maples, apple and plum trees, roses, tulips, lilies, crocuses, and bloodroot.

Each spring, the planting continued. The land bloomed, and the family came to call their beloved acres Lug-ins-land, which they translated as "Looking to the Land."[3] Charles even designed a three-block, bluffside walking trail so casual strollers could enjoy a view of the river. The story of the land's resurrection gained local fame. The *Burlington Hawkeye* boasted of the "bird's paradise" the Starkers had created: "Birds that were daily visitors in the long ago, and now but rarely seen, are found nesting on this idyllic spot, returning with the seasons, with the knowledge of security for themselves and their young."[4]

A tradition had begun.

Aldo's father, Carl Leopold, was the Starkers' nephew. He had made his way to Burlington from Liberty, Missouri, where his parents, Charles and Thusneld Runge Leopold, had settled after failing to make money in

Steven Brower

*The Starker home at Lug-ins-land, 101 Clay Street, was said to be "one of the handsomest in Burlington."[5] View from the south, circa 1878, showing the river.*

cattle. The Leopolds were also German immigrants of affluent heritage. Charles Leopold, like his brother-in-law Charles Starker, had worn many hats (including those of baker and brewer) in his efforts to make a good life in America for his seven children. The Leopolds aptly lived in Liberty, since Charles was an activist in the antislavery movement, and their home, it is thought, was a way station in the Underground Railroad.

When the Leopolds' youngest child, Carl, decided to study business, the Bryant and Stratton Business College of Burlington was a logical choice, since he could stay with the Starkers while he studied. After graduation, the strapping young Carl, sporting a handlebar mustache and often toting a shotgun, rambled through the Kansas and Nebraska territories as a traveling salesman. He helped farmers and ranchers lasso mile after mile of the swaying tallgrass into sections by selling them barbed wire, tools, and dry goods (roller skates were offered to their more adventurous offspring).

This free, vagabond life suited Carl. It gave him the opportunity he craved to roam the outdoors and do a little hunting. No town or desk roped him in.

But then he lassoed himself. Between business trips, he stayed once again with his Uncle Charles and Aunt Marie Starker, and he fell in love with their daughter. Home from her eastern boarding school, Clara Starker dressed in the height of fashion, talked in city slang, and was an avid sports fan. She had studied music, literature, and philosophy, and had an air of refinement about her. Lurking behind all that gentility, though, lay a lively, mischievous sense of humor. She loved the outdoors as much as her parents and was an exuberant ice skater (having won trophies for her prowess).

Carl and Clara were married on February 25, 1886. Carl quit traveling, and his father-in-law set him up in business with a partner, C. W. Rand (the son of Charles' partner E. W. Rand). Together they turned the Northwestern Furniture Company into the Rand Leopold Desk Company. The new Leopold family settled into the Starkers' back bedroom.

Marrying one's cousin was a lot more common then than now, but Clara and Carl's marriage still raised a few concerns. Nearly a year later, when their first child Aldo was born and seemed to be of sound mind

University of Wisconsin-Madison Archives (photo by Monford & Hill) X25 1070

*Aldo at age two or three with his dog (the first Spud, perhaps). Aldo's clothing shows how connected the Starker/Leopold family was to German custom. The Starker family visited Europe many times during the Burlington years.*

and body, everyone breathed a sigh of relief. Carl commented on more than one occasion: "Well, I guess we got by lucky."[6]

Aldo was christened Rand Aldo Leopold, after his father's business partner and a family friend named Aldo Sommers. (The "Rand" quickly slipped from the child's name, especially after the family had a falling-out with the Rands.) To honor the first child born in Lug-ins-land, the Starker/Leopold family planted a small red oak. It proved to be a symbol of Aldo's rich inheritance.

As soon as Aldo could walk, he was toddling beside his grandfather in the greenhouse and the yard, learning about the plants and songbirds. "Opa" (Grandpa) Starker would tell the boy stories and draw lifelike pictures of the animals and plants they saw.

In 1888, Aldo's sister Marie Luize was born, and in 1892, the Leopolds had another son, Carl Starker Leopold. Noise levels soared. Charles built his "liebchen" Clara her own house in the cow pasture behind the stables—at 111 Clay Street. The house, made of field stone and timber, was two and a half stories tall with deep bay windows and porches on both the front and the back. Aldo's youngest brother, Frederic, was born there in 1895.

The yard between the two homes became as busy as the Burlington bridge. It served as baseball diamond, skating rink, snowball battleground, and muddy track for stilt races in the spring. Aldo often led his brother Carl in daring escapades, including a tumble over the bluff on ice skates and a midnight snowball fight on the roof. More often than not, the Leopolds spent evenings in the parlor of the Big House reading stories aloud by the gaslight, devouring "Oma" (Grandma) Starker's German sweets, and singing songs from the Old Country accompanied by Clara on the piano.

Sundays in the spring and summer, weather permitting, the combined family packed the wagon for a picnic on the prairie or on the shore of one of the Illinois lakes.[7] "We might go to squirrel country," Marie recalled, "or . . . to bird country, or . . . over to the lakes and include a swim with the picnic. Aldo was usually out with his father walking, but we trailed along."[8]

As the chills of winter glazed in, gardening moved to the greenhouse, hunting became rabbit trapping, and the sleigh replaced the wagon, but the walks in the woods continued. These walks were lessons in woodscraft. Carl would hoist the smallest of his children onto his shoulders as he tramped, posing questions to his youngsters all the while. What animal lives under these limbs? What makes this rubbing on the bark and why? Why does this plant grow in this direction? "He would open up a decaying hollow log to show us the life dwelling inside, such as mice or large insects," remembered Frederic, the youngest. "He might show us where a mink had dug into a muskrat house to kill himself a muskrat for dinner. He

*University of Wisconsin-Madison Archives (photo by Monford & Hill) X25 1262*

*Carl Leopold in his outdoor gear with his hunting dog, Flick, about 1900.*

pointed out the old raccoon droppings, which might be identified by the content of wild grape seeds. We did not need to kill game to have an exciting afternoon in the swamp or field."[9]

Though all his siblings became amateur naturalists, Aldo took to woodscraft the most. "He was very much an outdoorsman," said Marie, "even in his extreme youth. He was always out climbing around the bluffs, or going down to the river, or going across the river into the woods."[10] The older he became, the more he set out for the fields on his own. Spud, his Irish terrier, was his sidekick as he wandered in search of berries, wildflowers, rabbits, and birds, or as he skinny-dipped in the creek. The dog was so much a part of his life that his classmates called Aldo "Spuddo."

On weekdays, Aldo walked about ten blocks southwest to Prospect

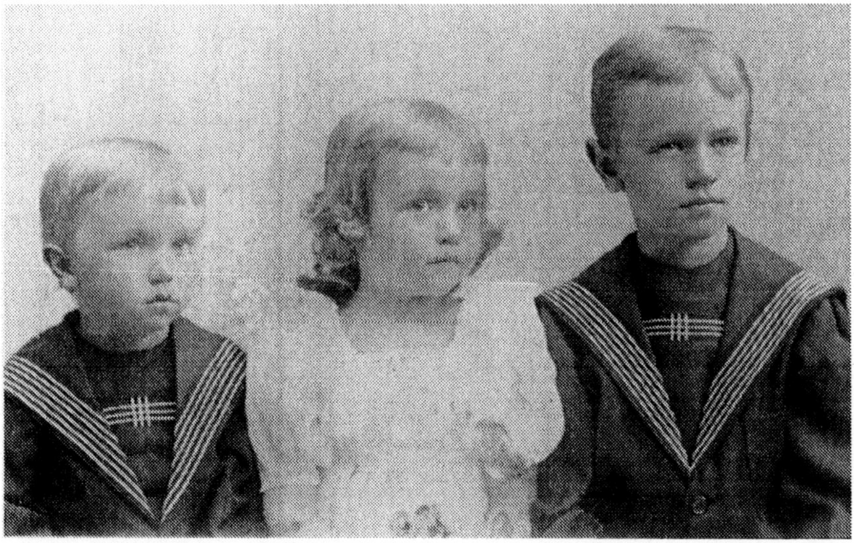

Des Moines County Historical Society

*The Leopold children in early 1895: (right to left) Aldo, age 8; Marie, age 6; Carl, Jr., age 3. Though Marie did not go hunting like her brothers, she too became a devoted naturalist. "We did have a very good time as a family, and a very busy time. No one ever said, 'What shall I do now?' We all had plenty of projects—especially Aldo."*[11]

Hill Elementary School. True to his naturalist yearnings, he was easily distracted by plants and birds he found in the woods on his way to school, even to the point of missing classes. His student records show, however, that his lessons didn't suffer: he ranked at the top of his elementary class. Though his first language was German, he had learned to speak and read English before entering school. As soon as possible, he shunned simple readers for the adventures of Daniel Boone, Hiawatha, and Jack London. He scanned his father's issues of *Outings* for stories of hunting and exploration, trying to pick up tips on surviving alone in the wilderness.

To balance out the education of self-reliance he was seeking, Aldo's mother Clara, who loved opera and literature, often recommended poems, plays, and novels to expand her son's reading repertoire. She enrolled him in classes to refine his social graces, including a dancing class.

The life of the rugged outdoorsman, though, remained Aldo's ideal. At a young age, probably before he started school, he began joining in on Carl's hunting trips. Long before dawn on Saturdays, dressing in many layers of wool and leather, he and his father would prepare for a long day outdoors. They whistled for the dogs and trudged downhill to the train station for a short trip to the Illinois side of the river. An efficient porter would call out their chosen stop for the day, and they'd depart to one of the hunting clubs along the tracks: Crystal Lake Hunt Club lay to the north and the Lone Tree Hunt Club to the south.

*University of Wisconsin–Madison Archives X25 2944*

*Aldo, second from left, did not enjoy being forced by his mother to learn the minuet, though later in life he did discover the advantages of being an accomplished dancer. Again, the European influence is obvious.*

*A humorous sketch of Carl Leopold, Sr. and the accompanying poem published in a Burlington journal edition called "Just for the Fun" (1913) show the reputation he had attained for his single-minded pursuit of hunting.* Des Moines County Historical Society

CARL LEOPOLD
He ships his desks the wide World 'round,
All over the Globe they are now found.
He enjoys that, of course,
But his real-truly-fun,
Is to slosh around in a swamp
With a Dog and a Gun.

Des Moines County Historical Society

*Crystal Lake Hunt Club. On his trips to his favorite hunting haunts, Carl generally took one son along at a time, leaving his wife and daughter at home. (There were no women members and few female visitors to the club at the time.)*

Aldo's memories of these trips were dear and treasured. "It would be difficult to exterminate from my mind," he wrote later in life, "the August landscape in which I took my first hunting trip, trailing after my father. The dried up cowtracks . . . looked to me like small chasms, and the purple-topped ironweeds like tall trees."[12]

On these first trips, Aldo carried a stick carved to imitate the weight and feel of a shotgun. The boy had to prove he could handle the stick carefully before Carl would trust him with a real gun. Carl never allowed his children to play with guns, not even toy ones. Safety was an absolute. "Never point a gun at anything you do not wish to kill,"[13] was his command. The shotguns he eventually gave his sons did not even have safety switches. He wanted them to depend on themselves for safety, not on their weapons.

Like many things for Carl, sportsmanship was a question of honor. It had a code of ethics that entailed rules and responsibilities. To ensure that he could find the birds he had shot, Carl never loaded a gun until after sunup. He avoided guns he thought were too powerful for sport (automatic or pump models). Instead, he opted for a double-barreled shotgun so he'd always have a second shot to kill any animal he wounded. Carl refused to hunt species whose numbers were dwindling; spring hunting was taboo as well, since species populations were especially vulnerable before the young were born. Instead of using feed or live baits, Carl carved decoys and depended on his knowledge of the animal. He wanted the hunting challenge to be as balanced as possible.

At the time, there were few hunting laws; market hunters and "game hogs" shot, clubbed, netted, trapped, and poisoned animals by the hundreds and thousands for their meat, feathers, or fur. Fish were even dynamited in streams. Yet Carl stuck to his guns, literally as well as figuratively, killing only what his family could eat before it spoiled. He spoke out in favor of hunting laws that would set bag limits and forbid the sale of game. He actively sought out news about the population counts of various species. Several American birds had already been hunted into extinction or near-extinction: the Carolina parakeet, the great auk, the heath hen, the Labrador duck, and the passenger pigeon.

Carl was not the only maverick in his fight against the unbridled waste of game hogs and market hunting. The same year Aldo was born, Theodore Roosevelt and George Bird Grinnell formed the Boone and Crockett Club, a big-game hunters' conservation society. A proud member, Carl saw Roosevelt as a model of heroic stature. With his own handlebar mustache and outdoorsman style of dress, he even took after Roosevelt in looks.

When Carl finally gave his eldest son a real shotgun, he forbade Aldo to shoot partridges or other birds at rest because it was not "sporting."

Wisconsin Department of Natural Resources

*A sample of the rampages that just a few market hunters in Wisconsin inflicted on a species population. In* A Sand County Almanac, *Leopold noted that in 1870, "a market gunner boasted in* American Sportsman *of killing 6,000 ducks in one season near Chicago."*[14]

Passing up such easy targets was no small test for the boy, especially since he was having no luck with those that moved.

One chilly winter Saturday, Aldo came upon a small patch of open water on a lake. If any ducks were still in the area, he figured, they would head for this water. He waited as the cold blasted him and his feet iced into numbness, but the sky yawned empty. Finally, as sunset stained the clouds, a lone black duck pitched downward. Aldo's shot shattered the silence, and the duck hit the snowy ice with a thud. The boy swelled with "unspeakable delight"[15] at his first kill. He was no longer a tag-along, but a true hunter.

Under his grandfather's tutelage, Aldo matured as a gardener and naturalist with the same enthusiasm. Charles Starker saw within each landscape the potential to become a natural work of art—he taught Aldo not only how to plant, prune, weed, and tend individual plant species, but also how to create an artistic design for a plot of land and experiment with different plantings to learn which plants thrived next to each other and which did not.

Aldo was a quick student, and early on, he demonstrated an aptitude for the observation and rendering of skills his grandfather modeled. He acquired a fondness for an expertly sharpened pencil and a lined notebook, becoming a notorious counter of birds. He tallied up species, colors, habits, and locations in his composition books. During his tenth summer, thirteen pairs of wrens nested in his yard. "We hatched one hundred and twenty young wrens," he wrote in his notebook. "I like wrens because they do more good than almost any other bird, they sing sweetly, they are very pretty, and very tame. I could have caught them many a time if I wanted to."[16]

University of Wisconsin–Madison Archives X25 2934

*One of Aldo's early drawings: Wren.*

By the age of eleven, Aldo had spotted thirty-nine bird species, listing them all in his composition book. (As many species were on the decline nationwide, Leopold might have had a very different life had he grown up someplace far from the Mississippi flyway.) These slim jottings were the beginnings of his long career as a nature chronicler.

In February 1900, only weeks after Aldo became a teenager, the natural rhythms of his life were abruptly shaken: Charles Starker died of a stroke. The *Burlington Democrat-Journal* wrote of this leading citizen, "It is not probable that there was another man in this community who was so generally and cordially esteemed alike by all classes of people."[17] Marie Starker died only a few months later.

The Big House, always filled with such energy, art, and warmth, suddenly echoed with hollowness.

# Ornithologists and Explorations

## 1901-1903

*Perhaps every youth needs an occasional wilderness trip . . .*

*"Flambeau,"* A Sand County Almanac

Aldo and his family moved back into the Big House the spring after his grandparents' deaths. Late in the summer, when the ragweed and goldenrod bloomed, Clara's hay fever hit with its annual vengeance. To comfort her, the Leopolds retreated to the northwoods resort they visited each summer.

The resort of Les Cheneaux embraced the outer edges of Marquette Island in Lake Huron. The island had not been logged recently, and a mix of tall pine, cedar, maple, fir, aspen, birch, and hemlock bristled over the land like fur. No roads and few trails cut through the woods. The Leopold cottage overlooked a mile-wide bay, where the sunsets were "indescribably beautiful."[1] Each day, a launch delivered groceries from the villages of Hessel and Cedarville on the Michigan coast.

The island enticed the young adventurer—here, he could fish, hunt, swim, sail, camp, and play Daniel Boone. While the rest of the family golfed or socialized with other wealthy guests from the lakeless Midwestern prairies,[2] Aldo explored every pine thicket, rocky rivulet, and turn of beach on the six-mile island, blazing trails and making intricate maps. Once he shot a "sachet kitten" near the clubhouse and carved this message on the boardwalk: "Aldo Leopold killed a skunk here on August 20, 1901."[3]

The Aldo Leopold Foundation

*Aldo in front of the clubhouse of Les Cheneaux with his catch and one of his favorite companions, Spud.*

(When the boardwalk was finally torn down, the resort owners saved the board.)

The "boys" in the family often packed up their canvas tents for week-long camp-outs by the lake. They would try to live off what they caught and picked. Aldo became a master at frying sourdough biscuits, cooking a wild stew over a smoking campfire, and using a Dutch oven.

North was Aldo's magical horizon. Frederic wrote: "In our young minds, we imagined that we were at the jumping-off place where to the north an endless wilderness extended to Hudson Bay and the arctic."[4] Aldo planned to someday paddle into the untouched lands of Canada, and he begged his father for a canoe. His father thought a rowboat suited them all just fine.

The Leopold Desks
BUILT ON HONOR TO ENDURE.

*Aldo's father, his great-grandfather Starker, and his great-great-grandfather Starker were all furniture dealers. When Carl Leopold, Sr., bought C. W. Rand's share of the Rand Leopold Desk Company in 1899, he gave his business a motto that reflected his ethics: "Built on Honor to Endure."*

*Des Moines County Historical Society*

*Clara Leopold, surrounded by her children, about 1901. Aldo and Marie stand in back; Carl and Frederic in front. Though Clara was devoted to all her children, Aldo was the runaway favorite. "We didn't hold it against him," said Frederic. "But her preference for him embarrassed Father a bit, and sometimes even embarrassed Aldo."*[5]

*University of Wisconsin-Madison Archives X25 1088*

By September 26, the Leopolds had ferried back to the mainland and boarded the "Hay Fever Special" to Chicago,[6] where they would catch the Chicago, Quincy & Burlington Railroad home. Carl had to return to the company he now owned—the Leopold Desk Company—and the children had to go to school.

Back at Burlington High, classes were overcrowded; students were given a choice of recitation times. Aldo selected the afternoons so the mornings would be his. He rose with the first light to roam the countryside, and on occasion, skipped the two-mile walk to school altogether, preferring the classroom of the woods.

Slim and sandy-haired, with serious, aqua eyes, Aldo stayed shyly silent in his courses. His marks did not suffer, except in math. (His weakness in this subject would come back to haunt him.) Miss Rogers drilled him in the rigors of the English language, and his biology teacher, in the complexities of the scientific classification system. With some coaxing from his mother, he also read a wide variety of works by scientists and novelists, philosophers and poets, historians and explorers. He noted descriptions of wildlife and landscapes, digesting changes over time. He also kept a notebook of inspiring quotations—Whittier, Tennyson, and Emerson made it to his best-loved list.

In 1902, Aldo inaugurated the first of a long line of ornithology journals. Using his prized *Handbook of Birds of Eastern North America* by Frank M. Chapman, he identified and described birds and tracked their habits:

> Lincoln's Sparrow: May 4-8. I found this little sparrow in a poplar thicket, feeding on the ground and occasionally springing into a low bush in the manner of a Swamp Sparrow, and giving off his song. . . . When alarmed, he would retreat into the thicket and sit motionless on an upper branch, watching the intruder. His most characteristic marks were narrow streaks and buffy lines along the sides of the throat.[7]

In these writings, Aldo honed his skills in observation and description.

Every day at 3:40 A.M., Aldo's classmate Edwin Hunger hauled his 160 newspapers up Clay Street and cut through the Leopold yard on his delivery route. There Aldo would be, staring up at the trees with his grandmother's opera glasses, his notebook in his lap. A puzzling sight, no doubt. Yet after a few meetings, Edwin expressed enough interest for Aldo to take Edwin under his wing, initiating him into the art and excitement of bird watching.

Spring migration drew the boys to water like finches to thistle. They caught the streetcar to Starr's Cave or rented a skiff to maneuver through the marshes of the Iowa bottomlands. Edwin was the "muscle man"—he rowed while Aldo sat in the back "perking up most lively when [Edwin] would

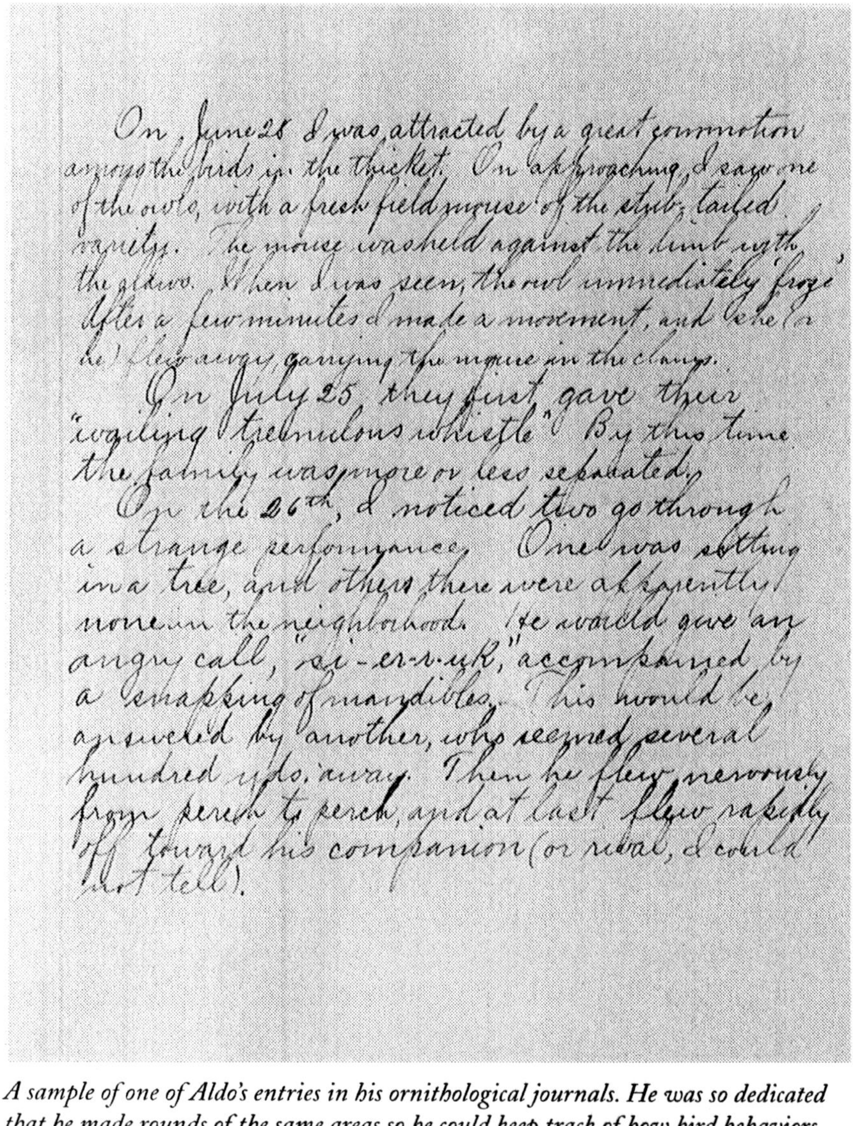
On June 25 I was attracted by a great commotion among the birds in the thicket. On approaching, I saw one of the owls, with a fresh field mouse of the stub-tailed variety. The mouse was held against the limb with the claws. When I was seen, the owl immediately "froze." After a few minutes I made a movement, and she (or he) flew away, carrying the mouse in the claws.

On July 25 they first gave their "wailing tremulous whistle." By this time the family was more or less separated.

On the 26th, I noticed two go through a strange performance. One was sitting in a tree, and others there were apparently none in the neighborhood. He would give an angry call, "si-er-r-uk," accompanied by a snapping of mandibles. This would be answered by another, who seemed several hundred yds. away. Then he flew nervously from perch to perch, and at last flew rapidly off toward his companion (or rival, I could not tell).

University of Wisconsin–Madison Archives X25 2933

*A sample of one of Aldo's entries in his ornithological journals. He was so dedicated that he made rounds of the same areas so he could keep track of how bird behaviors changed over time and according to situation. He would sometimes make guesses about reasons for specific behaviors and then continue to watch to confirm or disprove his theories.*

sneak the skiff into some narrow slough."[8] The boys each kept a separate tally of new species they sighted, and Aldo was consistently in the lead. This competition did not taint their friendship. For Edwin, Aldo was "an inspiring

Des Moines County Historical Society

*Starr's Cave, one of the natural formations near Burlington, and the site of bird-watching adventures for Aldo and Edwin.*

fellow bird watcher, the finest and truest friend I've ever had."[9]

In the summer of 1903, the Leopolds skipped their usual vacation at Les Cheneaux in favor of exploring the new national parks in the Rocky Mountains. After camping in Estes Park, Aldo and his father left the rest of the family behind for a pack-horse trip north to hunt big game. The sight of Yellowstone National Park's bison and geysers and a breakdown of one of the wagons set the pace for Aldo's adventures. On August 31, he wrote in his journal, "Woke at 1 o'clock a.m., bear had stampeded horses and was now walking across the meadow near camp. Us boys caught the horses ½ mile away and met guide with new wagon and again went to bed. ¼ inch of ice in morning."[10] Two days later, a bear succeeded in raiding their provisions, devouring the bacon, sausage, prunes, sugar, and cheese. Snow slowed them down, their guide fell ill, and their luck at hunting dipped to its lowest.

All this did little to dampen the teen's spirits. He added 40 new species to his bird lists, bringing his total to 261. Aldo's first taste of wilderness inspired him to confide in his journal that he could think of "no better possible vacation."[11]

# The Naturalist Out East
## 1903-1905

*I heard of a boy once who was brought up an atheist.*
*He changed his mind when he saw*
*there were a hundred-odd species of warblers,*
*each bedecked like to a rainbow,*
*and each performing . . . thousands of miles of migration*
*about which scientists wrote wisely but did not understand.*

*"Goose Music,"* A Sand County Almanac

For decades, Carl Leopold had watched rafts of pine logs swaddled together like organ pipes, from a block to a half-mile in length, float down the Mississippi from the northern forests of Minnesota, Wisconsin, and Michigan. By the turn of the century, these rafts had dwindled in frequency and length. Most of the two- to five-hundred-year-old white pine forests that had surrounded the Great Lakes and the eastern seaboard had been sliced to stubble, and logging companies were abandoning these leavings for the untouched forests of the West. Carl couldn't help but notice. His business was built on wood, and if wood supplies ran out, so would his source of income. Greed and waste were the razors of the lumber trade, and Carl knew well that the forests of the West would fall to their blades if the public did not protest.

Just as he monitored the number of ducks and geese he hunted, Carl believed in guarding the number of trees cut. So, despite his longing for Aldo to follow him in the family business, he unintentionally primed his

Minnesota Historical Society

*The steamer "Lydia Vansant" with a log raft on the upper Mississippi around the turn of the century.*

eldest for a very different profession. Carl scanned newspapers and outdoors magazines seeking forest news, expounding on his findings to his eldest. Edwin Hunger tagged along on some of Carl's outings with his sons, and described them as "lectures on the move" in which the boys learned "much about the woods in general and how they should be managed and preserved."[1]

While Aldo was in elementary school, Presidents Benjamin Harrison and Grover Cleveland set aside millions of acres out West in forest reserves. Members of the lumber, mining, and ranching industries responded with outrage; they wanted no limits on their use of public lands. But increasingly, concerned citizens were pushing for national laws to protect the remaining forests. One prophet in the fray was John Muir. He preached a gospel of preservation: Stop the wasteful destruction and let the forests manage themselves. Cut only populous common trees, and then only sparingly and carefully, "for every right use."[2]

Working with the preservationists were others who called themselves conservationists. They promoted a platform of moderation and managed "wise use" as the best path to forest and game species survival. A dedicated

Yosemite National Park Research Library

*Theodore Roosevelt and John Muir in 1903 at Yosemite.*

USDA Forest Service, Grey Towers National Historic Landmark, Milford, PA

*Gifford Pinchot, about 1910.*

Photographic Archives of the Arnold Arboretum, Harvard University

*Botanist Charles Sprague Sargent, director of the Arnold Arboretum at Harvard University.*

outdoorsman, Theodore Roosevelt was a leader in this fight. Alongside him stood Gifford Pinchot, a Yale graduate who had studied European forest management in Germany and France. Pinchot imported to the United States the idea of utilitarian forestry—the scientific management of the tree count and the forest range "for the greatest good for the greatest number over the long run."[3]

Though the reserved forests were now held in public trust, no official system had been established to oversee them. Pinchot argued for a full cadre of trained foresters to manage the forests so lumbering, mining, and grazing could be allowed on a regulated basis, with monocultural replantings of commercially useful trees to make the timber last forever. In contrast, John Muir, the botanist Charles Sprague Sargent of Harvard University's Arnold Arboretum, and Editor Robert Underwood Johnson of *Century* magazine favored surrounding the reserves (especially the irreplaceable old-growth forests, such as the California redwood groves) with army troops to protect them from timber poachers and industrialists.

Pinchot's views won out. President Cleveland selected Pinchot to oversee the Division of Forestry in the Department of Agriculture, and in 1900, the Pinchot family donated money to Yale University to start a forestry school. When Vice President Theodore Roosevelt became president, he signed millions more acres out West into national protection and transferred all the forest reserves into Pinchot's care. The United States Forest Service stepped out of theory into reality.

When Aldo heard of Yale's new forestry training program and the new Forest Service, answers to the questions he had about his future fell into place. And that place was in the woods.

Aldo, considering the advice of his mother and a family friend, believed he'd have little chance of getting into Yale without an eastern boarding-school education. (Clara wanted him to have an education out East, as she had.) Carl defended Iowa's offerings. He still had visions of his eldest joining him in the Leopold Desk Company. Aldo and Clara prevailed, and in the middle of his junior year (after his trip West), Aldo transferred from Burlington High School to the Lawrenceville School, a respected college preparatory boarding school in New Jersey. In a reference letter to the Lawrenceville headmaster, the principal at Burlington High School wrote: "He is as earnest a boy as we have in school. . . . painstaking in his work. . . . Moral character above reproach."[4]

Six days before his seventeenth birthday, the quiet, exemplary student boarded a train for the small country town tucked between Princeton and Trenton. No doubt Aldo had his private concerns about the move. He was half a year behind the rest in his studies; he knew none of his classmates; and upon arrival, he noticed quickly that amongst his East Coast counterparts, his accent and manners said loud and clear, "I'm from out West."

The Lawrenceville School

*An early 1900s photograph of one section of the grounds of the Lawrenceville School, showing the Cleve and Griswold Houses, which were student residences, and the chapel, to the right.*

Aldo protected himself from the teasing of his classmates with a holier-than-thou attitude and a little sarcasm. He studied hard and by himself, and when he wrote letters home, he described his companions' unscholarly attitudes and pursuits—smoking, drinking, sports, and girls—with contempt.

Clara depended upon these letters for doses of cheer. She checked her mailbox daily. A dutiful son, Aldo wrote nearly 10,000 pages home during his school and early career years. The lengthy descriptions of his days served as an apprenticeship in the craft of writing. He experimented with styles, tones, and formats, and his mother responded with constructive suggestions. These letters drove a writing habit so deep into his life it would never be uprooted.

Though determined to succeed at Lawrenceville, Aldo couldn't stand being caged in the school's study halls and classrooms for too long. He packed his writing pad and notebook out into the fields, and within less than a month of his arrival, he had drawn a map of the countryside for ten miles in all directions, assigning names to the landmarks: Fern Woods, Ash Swamp, the Boulders. Nearly every day, he hiked to a favorite haunt and stayed for at least an hour. His old habit of cutting classes returned.

Even so, Aldo caught up to his classmates in most, but not all, courses. He wrote home on April 8, 1904: "My dear Mama, You probably know from my report that I have flunked Geometry, whether or not I have Elocution I do not know as yet."[5] The school responded with supervised study periods, to keep him inside and paying proper attention. Thus imprisoned, he sought to bring the outside in. He tended an indoor garden of potted pansies, Boston ferns, and some native species, such as hepatica, which he had brought back from his tramps.

In his choice of lectures, Aldo sought subjects that dealt with the outdoors. After one class lecture given by a Native American (whose name he did not mention), he wrote home: "Some words and phrases which I have never heard before impressed me greatly. He said, 'Nature is the gate to the Great Mystery.'"[6]

Aldo seized every opportunity to promote the cause of conservation. He sprung traps in the woods and revived dying fish from a drained campus pond. In a speech contest, he presented a case in favor of forest preservation. If the forests are destroyed, he warned, "Nature's balance" will be overturned and "changes in climate will follow."[7] As proof, he described the fate of Spain:

> She was once the most powerful nation on earth. The fertility of

her fields was second to none; her people were prosperous. But in her greed for gain the mountain forests were destroyed, as ours are being destroyed today. And now this same Spain lies blistering under the heat of a tropical sun, a rainless desert.[8]

In the spring of 1904, Aldo heard of some hunters breaking the newly issued hunting laws and killing 150 ducks apiece. He assured his father that he would work to end such slaughter. "When my turn comes to have something to say and do against it . . . I'm sure nothing in my power will be lacking to the good cause."[9]

As time passed, Aldo's time at Lawrenceville was not all spent in such serious pursuits. His dining mates, Henry Van Dyke, George Orr, "Ham" Drummond, and "Poittie" Page, made it their business to loosen up "the Naturalist." Even Aldo could not withstand their constant teasing and shenanigans without shrugging off some of his disdain and showing a sense of humor. Gradually, he was allowed into the inner circle, joining in on some of the jokes, pranks, and parties. Against his parents' wishes (a big step for Aldo), he joined the cross-country track team with the "boys." The fellows then began asking to accompany him on his tramps. It only took one trip each for Aldo to gain their respect.

Living frugally, Aldo held on affectionately to his well-worn boots and tramping clothes, upholding his ideals of independence and self-reliance. On each field outing, he toted along his birding journal and Asa Gray's *Manual of Botany*, to identify leaves and wildflowers. Plants had suddenly become as interesting as birds to him, and he began to see how wild species affected each other. He noted in his journal that since skunk cabbage stinks and blooms early, it attracts insects before many other plants; thus it also attracts the insect-eating phoebes. Nothing in the woods was unworthy of Aldo's notice: from yellow adder's tongue to bloodroot, to Acadian flycatchers, crawfish, bullfrogs, and muskrats. Though he treasured his shotgun, he felt no inclination to use it on his tramps, and he wrote to his father in the spring of 1904:

I hope you and Carl . . . will enjoy many of these fine Spring days over in the swamps, just *seeing* things; indeed, I cannot imagine

*Aldo's school portrait at Lawrenceville in 1905. He had not completely left behind his "no nonsense" appearance. The dean described him as a "particularly fine fellow, sturdy, intelligent, and well balanced."*[10]

wanting to kill anything now when there is so much to see and appreciate out of doors. [11]

The amateur naturalist had come to the point in his observations where he could interpret various bird calls, and when some species didn't fly according to their normal migration patterns, he missed them. In the villages around the school, the name of Aldo Leopold was renowned among birding enthusiasts. Professors at Princeton and members of a bird-watching club asked him to serve as a judge for their joint essay contest.

In his coursework, Aldo had so surpassed some of his classmates that they labeled him a "shark."[12] He darted gracefully through his final exams and the college entrance exams, and graduated in June 1905.

Aldo returned to Burlington for the summer full of confidence. At Les Cheneaux that year, he ignored the usual "fussing game" of dances,[13] parties, and golfing events, and pursued his solitary tramps across the island. The rest of the Les Cheneaux college set found Aldo's pinings for the woods unfathomable, and he became known as "Adam,"[14] the original man. His brother Frederic remarked, "He did not think he was cut from the common cloth, and he wasn't."[15]

# Women and Wise Use
# 1905-1909

*Education, I fear,*
*is learning to see one thing by going blind to another.*
*"Clandeboye,"* A Sand County Almanac

New Haven, Connecticut, where the Yale campus stretched its ivy-hung halls, was a far larger, busier, less countrified place than Lawrenceville. The Yale Forest School granted only graduate degrees, so Aldo enrolled in the Sheffield Scientific School on the Yale campus for his undergraduate studies. The college offered students a program of preparatory courses for the Forest School: physics, chemistry, German, mechanical drawing, and analytical geometry.

In a room at 400 Temple Street, Aldo set up a lifestyle as frugal and self-reliant as he had in Lawrenceville. He stayed loyal to his plan for studying, working out in the gymnasium, and running cross-country track, while attending a variety of special lectures and expanding his reading list. In his reading as in his running, he covered great distances in a short time. He read *Outdoor Pastimes of an American Hunter* by Theodore Roosevelt alongside the Bible; books on forestry accompanied the works of Longfellow, Emerson, Thoreau, Cicero, and others. A tome inspiring "much interest and surprise"[1] was Charles Darwin's *Vegetable Mould and Earthworms*. (A year or so earlier, he had read *A Naturalist's Voyage Around the World* and proclaimed it "very instructive."[2])

Aldo had far less time for tramping now. The countryside was farther away, and his four- to seven-a-week treks dwindled to one or two. Though he enjoyed the outings just as much, they were becoming a hobby rather than a way of life. His courses were more challenging, and he was beguiled by Ivy League activities and a new group of friends. Descriptions of football games and college parties began to fill his letters. He even let his sister Marie arrange a Christmastime schedule of dances and social engagements for him in Burlington, and then surprised himself by enjoying it all. Women, many of them Marie's friends, had entered his domain of interest with a flourish, and his dancing lessons finally proved useful. Ham, from Lawrenceville, teased Aldo for his new fancies: "You have decayed into what I used to be—the lover with his ballad, the devoted sweetheart; the passionate letter-writer. Ah me!"[3]

Once Aldo adjusted to his classwork and the whirlwind of his new social life, he volunteered at the nearby YMCA. Yale students often took disadvantaged children under their wings. Following this tradition, Aldo struck up a friendship with a poor Jewish boy, Benjamin Jacobsky. The contrast between the good fortune of Aldo's life and the misfortune of Bennie's became painfully obvious. Bennie's life had been hard in every way that Aldo's had been easy: Bennie's parents took little notice of their son and thrived on disagreements. Aldo led Bennie off to the woods for tramps and picnics—new experiences for the city-docks-bound boy. His relationship with Bennie gave Aldo a new perspective on his life and on life in general.[4] He wrote home:

> Even though the course of one [person's life] has been smooth, and that of a second miserable, is *that* a cause for sorrow to the first? I take it not so, but in double measure a cause for *action* to him. It is deeds, not tears, that *shall*, and someday *will*, give to the oppressed of the earth their due! Therefore let us *rejoice* in the June and *work*.[5]

That summer, the changes in Aldo became even more apparent to his family. He took to the fussing game as eagerly as the rest of the college gang, settling his attentions on a Miss Gretchen Miller. He added a twist to his serenading that his rivals could not match. As his father had finally bought him a canoe, he was able to take the women in his life (including his mother and sister) on moonlit rides.

Once he returned to school, Aldo forsook his penny-pinching ways, practical pants, and tramping boots for new Brooks Brothers suits, tailored shirts, and expensive dress shoes. The new dandy applied to a fraternity and joined the Forester's Club. The busier his social life and class schedule became, the less Aldo tramped and the lonelier his letters home sounded. When at last he was able to enroll in some Forest School courses, he hunkered down like a half-starved lion to a kill. He lost weight; he strained his eyes; he had trouble sleeping. He was trying to do too much—to be the student, the athlete, the social activist, the socialite, and in his spare time, the naturalist. His letters again reflected his belief that he had done nothing to deserve all the good things in his life, and that therefore he was duty-bound to give back all he could.

The Aldo Leopold Foundation

*Aldo on the dock at Les Cheneaux in 1907.*

When Carl wrote to say that he was working on Iowa legislation for a new system of hunting regulations, Aldo was disappointed that he could not be part of his father's admirable work. Aldo once more wrote to reassure his father that as soon as he was able he would do his best for "our poor ducks and other game in return for what they have been and will be to me."[6] He also confided that he missed his father: "We have always been in the woods together, we understand each other there, and you are still and by far my best companion in the open."[7]

That was enough to convince his hardworking father to take some time off for a backpacking trip in the Green Mountains of Vermont in that summer of 1907. Carl, Sr., came East and found his eldest son weary inside and out: "worse than I have ever seen him."[8] The trip together was the rest cure they both needed.

Afterwards, Aldo trekked on to the Yale Forest School Camp in the Pocono Mountains of Pennsylvania. His time spanned between working with his hands and with numbers: chopping and thinning, surveying and mapping. Nature was gradually becoming for him something that could be measured, managed, and put to human use. Using mathematical deductions, he could figure out whether a forest needed thinning or replanting, and how many boards it could produce.

USDA Forest Service, Grey Towers National Historic Landmark, Milford, PA

*A scene from the Yale Forest School Camp in Milford, Pennsylvania, the summer after Aldo attended it.*

Just as Aldo was expanding his notion of forests, the field of American forestry was expanding its domain. President Roosevelt more than doubled the acreage of the forest reserve system—from 63 to 150 million acres. In 1907, Gifford Pinchot renamed the reserves the National Forests. With this new term, he defined his position—the forests were to be used, not reserved.

Pinchot had won the contest over the fate of the forests, and in many ways, so had the industrialists. Pinchot refused to place an upper limit on the amount of board feet to be cut from the forests, claiming, "The conservation movement has development for its first principle."[9] However, Pinchot reserved for his forest managers the authority to use scientific principles of management to make decisions about each forest's use.

He promoted his aims as both practical and democratic. In his view, a forest's main purpose was to be a tree lot for timber "for the benefit of the Community and the Home Builder."[10] To gain support from western ranchers and sheep herders, Pinchot also allowed grazing within the forests. The preservationists fought these concessions as infringements on the forests' beauty and integrity. But to the public, these aesthetic and philosophical arguments didn't ring as true as the clinking of coins from timber sales and grazing permits.

Aldo's views, like those of many of his fellow foresters, were split. He could see both sides of the argument—wise use on the one hand, and the preservation of beauty and nature on the other. For the time being, however, he bought Pinchot's program.

In the fall of 1907, Aldo entered his third year of classes at the Sheffield School. Any class that did not directly relate to forest management bored him; plant morphology was the worst. "You sit for four hours a week," he wrote, "squinting through a microscope at a little drop of mud all full of wiggly bugs and things, and then draw pictures of them and label [them] with ungodly names. . . . One cannot help wondering what the *Cyanophycens oscillatorius* has to do with raising timber."[11] So he partied, skipped classes, and played the fussing game.

The dean wrote to Burlington to complain. Reprimands from home had little effect. Just a month after his twenty-first birthday, the school put him on probation—one more strike and he was out.

Clara put her foot down. "It is time to call a halt," she wrote Aldo. "Nothing short of a complete readjustment of your present life to your old ideas will put you on a safe road."[12]

Aldo snapped to attention at his mother's order. He cut extra activities and quit his partying. In the end, he managed to pass his final exams and graduate.

The next fall, Aldo returned to New Haven as a master's student in the Yale Forest School. Having proven himself ready to join Pinchot's

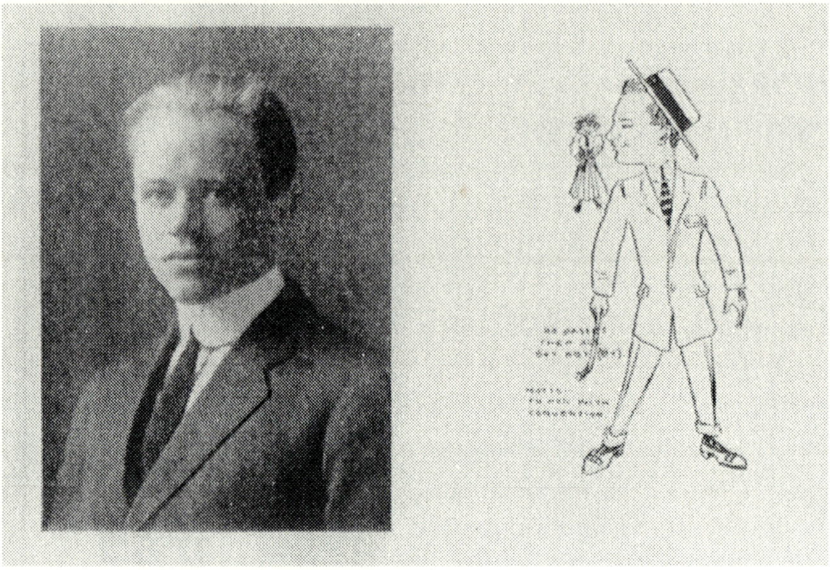

"To hell with convention."

Yale University Library: Manuscripts and Archives

*The Sheffield Scientific School's 1908 yearbook portrait and caricature of Aldo, mocking his newfound enthusiasm for clothes and women.*

elite corps, he settled down to a diet of forest law, forest regions, lumbering, and timber management and practice. He began to think of forests as he was taught—in terms of numbers, planks, and dollars. He even made a little money off his study techniques. He drew a chart of tree species that made them easy to identify, and had it printed. His initial printing sold out, his first publishing success.

Aldo wasn't completely comfortable with the changes he noticed in himself. He wrote to his friend Ham, "I'm getting narrow as a clam with all this technical work."[13] His new focus on numbers didn't make mathematics any easier for him. He admitted to his mother on January 20, 1909, "I have made a mistake in a lot of my calculations in Timber Testing (done with great care) and I will have to do them over."[14] Aldo became a quick convert to a new work-saving invention—the slide rule (not to mention the typewriter and the camera).

In February, Aldo graduated with a master's degree. Only two hoops remained: a field stint and the civil service exams.

The Aldo Leopold Foundation

*Though attentive to style, Aldo still did not conform. In this photo of the 1909 graduating class of Yale foresters, he is in front in the light, striped suit.*

Aldo's fieldwork position was set in Doucette, Texas, a land of mosquitoes and snakes, where the "grub-shack" set a table of "beans, goat's meat and apricots."[15] Though living in a tent, Aldo made himself at home, putting up a bookshelf and planting a vegetable garden. Charles Starker's legacy had found a receptive spirit in his grandson. Aldo wrote to his mother:

> I guess there is no doubt about it; I am just as much a born farmer as you are, and some day when I retire (?) I am going to own me a patch of ground and a hoe, and live the happy life. . . . I shall get me in addition a woodlot, with squirrel and partridges and Turkeys, and some fields with horses and quail and innumerable dogs.[16]

After packing up his tent and passing the civil service exams, Aldo listed his preferences for a forest assignment (out of the six districts) in this order: District 3 (the Southwest), District 5 (the Sierras), and District 6 (Oregon and Washington). The more isolated, the better. He was still looking for the chance to live the life of the self-reliant explorer. He wrote home that a friend had said, "I'd rather be a [Forest] Supervisor than be the King of England." Aldo added: "I'm beginning to agree with him."[17]

# A Cowboy in Love

## 1909-1912

*The Busy Season*

*There's many a crooked rocky trail*
*that we'd like straight and free,*
*There's many a mile of forest isle*
*where a fire sign ought to be,*

*There's many a pine tree on the hills,*
*in soothe they are tall and straight,*
*But what we want to know is this—*
*what will they estimate?*

*There's many a cow-brute on the range,*
*and her life is wild and free,*
*But can she look at you and say*
*she's paid the grazing fee?*

*All this and more, it's up to us—*
*and say, boys, Can we do it?*
*I have just three words to say*
*and they are these: TAKE TO IT!*

The Carson Pine Cone, *1911*[1]

Twenty-two-year-old Aldo Leopold arrived in Albuquerque, New Mexico Territory, in July 1909, burning with the "fervor of a sawdust evangelist."[2] The Forest Service had sent him to his first choice—District 3, encompassing the twenty-one forests of the South and Southwest. His duties were outlined in his manual: preserve a perpetual supply of timber for home industries, prevent destruction of forest cover (which regulates the flow of streams), and protect local industries from unfair competition in the use of forest and range.[3]

The district chief was Arthur Ringland, a stocky, energetic Yale graduate only a few years older than Leopold. Ringland sensed the new graduate's enthusiasm and assigned him to the wildest lands in the district—the Apache National Forest in Arizona Territory. The land had originally belonged to the Apache Nation, but in 1886, the U.S. Army forced most of the members onto a nearby reservation. This left but a few ranchers, farmers, and miners in the region.

The forest headquarters rested in Springerville, Arizona, a two-day stagecoach ride from the last railroad stop. No automobiles carved tire treads over these plateaus and canyons. Travel was by foot, horse, or mule.

Forest Assistant Leopold, the newest greenhorn among many, wasted no time in purchasing a feisty gray stallion called Jiminy Hicks, a saddle, a rope, and a few good roping lessons. Within the month, he also acquired pistols and a "rubber butt plate"[4] for those long days in the saddle.

Forest History Society, Durham, NC (photo by J. D. Guthrie)

*Leopold in 1910 with his dog Flick. The purchase of his cowboy accoutrements put a squeeze on the young forester's budget of $83.33 a month. An SOS to Burlington brought money to tide him over.*

The rubber plate came in handy since Aldo put in a good deal of time astride Jiminy Hicks. Throughout July and the beginning of August, Leopold inspected trees, marked them for cutting, planted seed plots, fixed fences, and met the other rangers. Working under Supervisor John D. Guthrie, Aldo contributed his two bits on policy decisions about grazing permits, water rights, and timber sales. Guthrie's long hours and dedicated stance inspired the young ranger.

The simplicity of life on the range, where one had to live out of a pack, made Leopold feel tough and free. On his own time, he hunted, mapped out the forest for himself, climbed mountains, and tested trout streams. To his mother, he confided:

> Why I wouldn't trade it for anything else under the sun. Please don't think that every time I tell you of having 'laid out' overnight or doing a full days work that I am to be pitied on that account. Jiminy Crickets—it's part of the job. . . . Ten times as much roughing it would not be too big a price to pay for the privilege of wearing a flannel shirt and of not being obliged [to] fight society and all the forty 'leven kinds of Tommyrot that includes.[5]

When assigned to headquarters duties, Leopold read and passed many midnight hours discussing game, conservation philosophies, forests, women, and baseball with his bunkhouse brothers. The rangers slept in the bachelor quarters—"lang 'dobe" (the long adobe)—and lived off biscuits and huevos rancheros (red beans, bacon, scrambled eggs, and cheese). Ranger Leopold occasionally broke the monotony by bagging a duck or two.

The Apache land, with its dry lines and sharp edges, enchanted the young forester. Mountains covered in ponderosa pines descended to flower-spangled meadows. Piñon and juniper tinged the air with their scents of bitter fruit. Cottonwoods, sycamores, and willows edged craggy river canyons. Aldo mused in poetry: "Ho, the Mesa of the Angels, has it never called to you?"[6]

Wildlife still had its say in the wild lands of the Apache. Mule deer, turkeys, pronghorn antelope, ptarmigans, and mountain sheep roamed the colored cliffs and sand plains. Back East, white-tailed deer, wild turkeys, and Canada geese were nearly extinct. Bison, elk, antelope, and other game (in addition to grizzlies and cougars) had been driven from the lands around the Mississippi and were now growing scarce out West as well. President Roosevelt had established fifty-one game refuges before leaving office, but many preservationists *and* conservationists feared the number was far too few to pull the declining species back from the precipice of extinction.

Following Roosevelt's lead, Forest Assistant Leopold tinkered with a plan for a game refuge in the Blue Mountains, a project of which Supervisor Guthrie approved. In the meantime, Leopold and the rest of the rangers kept up a steady war against wolves, mountain lions, and grizzlies—the predators that ate the game species the foresters wanted to protect. The foresters shot, trapped, or poisoned these "varmints," earning bounties for their successes.

In August, Leopold was chosen to replace the director of a reconnaissance crew. The team's job was to pace out the eastern edge of the forest and map it into forty-acre sections. At the team's disposal were compasses, pace counters, barometers, and notebooks. The maps had to detail the natural and artificial features of each section, as well as the number and types of trees growing there. Leopold led a shorthanded crew of two local lumbermen and three foresters. He was to give out assignments, check surveys and calculations, do some pacing, and make sure his men got along.

Aldo's Achilles' heel quickly tripped him up. His calculations didn't add up, so his section maps didn't line up. He wasted days rechecking his maps, and the crew fell behind schedule. He refused help from the experienced men, abandoned camp for an inspection of a game refuge along the Blue River, and left the men with dwindling rations.

The crew didn't wait around for him. Once Leopold caught up with them, they snarled with anger and disgust. Aldo wrote to his sister:

> Two of the men, Lumberjacks to boot, began to grumble this morning about the 'hard life.' Why damn their whining souls, wait till it begins to snow. That will take the conceit out of them.

> . . . It looks as if it [will] take all the tact and patience I can raise to hold the party together until I finish the job.[7]

The crew did hold together, no thanks to Leopold. Rather than purchase supplies, he scrimped on rations and hunted, forcing the men to sit on the ground and eat venison cooked over an open fire. More than once, he threw them all even further behind schedule by chasing after poachers and predators. One particular afternoon, Leopold and another crew member spotted a wolf and her pups crossing the river. They shot into the pack and then scrambled down the rocks to see what they had done.

One pup was crippled and trying to crawl away. The old mother wolf lay snapping and growling. Aldo baited her with his rifle, and the wolf lunged at him, snatching it in her teeth. The men backed away, but kept their eyes on her, watching her die. Many years later, Leopold wrote:

> We reached the old wolf in time to watch a fierce green fire dying in her eyes. I realized then, and have known ever since, that there was something new to me in those eyes—something known only to her and to the mountain.[8]

The scene haunted Aldo, though he couldn't figure out why. It took him a long time to understand the implications of what he had done.

Despite its leader, the surveying crew managed to finish the job before the snows came. Although his crew had just barely finished on time, and the cost of the venture had soared far beyond the budgeted amount, Aldo's head had swollen with power. He boasted to his mother: "Millions of acres, billions of feet of timber, all vast amounts of capital—why it's fun to twiddle them around in your fingers, especially when you consider your very modest amount of experience."[9]

The reconnaissance fiasco, however, had not played its last scene. Before handing in his report, Leopold discovered his baseline calculations were still off by 1,000 feet. It took until mid-February 1910—two months beyond the due date—to recalculate all the maps. Once he completed the report, the attacks on it and on the mission's leader ensued. Poorly organized. Confusing. Incomplete. Too expensive. Incompetent leadership. Easily sidetracked. Hasty decisions. The criticisms were so severe it seemed Leopold might be kept from heading that summer's survey. Arthur Ringland demanded an investigation.

Aldo welcomed the inquiry, thinking it would clear him. It didn't. One member testified, "In my opinion, Mr. Leopold considered the Apache reconnaissance a picnic party instead of a serious matter."[10] Fortunately for Aldo, one student member weakly defended him, "I can remember . . . no important point where Mr. Leopold was at fault, except that he was green and inexperienced."[11] This, in the end, was the investigation's conclusion. Leopold would be given another chance.

That spring, the West was as dry as a tumbleweed. Five large fires and a number of smaller ones roared across the Apache and nearby forests. For the first time, Leopold and his companions faced the forester's biggest enemy: fire. They stood the test—with sweat, muscle, and nerve, they held the lines.

Rains came in June, bringing some relief.

By mid-July 1910, Leopold and a team even greener than he were

University of Wisconsin–Madison Archives X25 1860

*On Leopold's second surveying trip, the crew grumbled about the cooks and the grub. The timber cruisers buried a loaf of bread in protest, nicknaming the camp "Camp Indigestion."[12] Leopold is second from the right.*

sent forth to begin surveying. J. Howard Allison, a reconnaissance expert, joined the group to evaluate Leopold's leadership. Aldo wrote to his mother, "It's sure interesting to be the villain."[13]

Allison stayed with the men for a month, long enough to see that Leopold had learned from his experience and was handling the crew and calculations competently. By November, the "timber cruisers" returned to headquarters triumphant, having surveyed one-third of the Apache National Forest.

Though far more interested in outdoors duties than in office records or procedures, Forest Assistant Leopold kept painstaking notes of all his actions. He invented new ways to document and track forest data. "I am sure a dumhead [sic] when it comes to memorizing routine procedures," he commented to his father, "so it's up to me to be useful in some way, I guess."[14] His suggestions and innovative reports impressed Chief Ringland.

In the spring of 1911, Ringland summoned Leopold to District 3

USDA National Agriculture Library

*Arthur C. Ringland, District Forester, Albuquerque, New Mexico, 1912.*

The Aldo Leopold Foundation

*Estella Bergere in 1913.*[15] *She was a twenty-year-old first-grade teacher when Aldo met her. Aldo described her in a letter to his mother: "She must be extremely beautiful, since I do not think she would be called especially pretty. She is very dark, her hair has a reddish glint should you ever see it exactly right, she has very beautiful eyes, [an] aquiline nose, and a very fine mouth. Her voice is very low, she is slender and not tall, and dresses extremely well but very simply."*[16]

Headquarters in Albuquerque for a meeting of reconnaissance leaders and a temporary work assignment. Ringland wanted to decide on an appropriate new position for his now-seasoned ranger. The best option seemed to be the Chiricahua National Forest, near the Arizona/Mexico border.

One March afternoon, Chief Ringland and Ranger Leopold were in a drugstore in Albuquerque when two of the seven lovely Bergere sisters strolled in. Arthur introduced Aldo to the women. A few weeks later, the sisters invited the two foresters to their ranch in Santa Fe for a cotillion. The bachelors readily accepted.

As the two men approached the hacienda, boisterous melodies from Spanish guitars and laughter floated on the dry evening breeze. Young señoritas wove in and out of the crowd, carrying bird-shaped paper lanterns and presenting them to the señors in exchange for dances.

On the third dance, Estella Bergere shyly handed Aldo her parrot. Señorita Bergere had made a new conquest.

Perceiving Aldo's attraction to Miss Bergere, Ringland changed his mind about the Chiricahua and assigned Leopold to the Carson National Forest, the closest forest to Santa Fe—and to Estella.

Within a few weeks, Leopold boarded the narrow-gauge railroad which was "slower 'n a burro and about as sorry,"[17] for Antonito, in Colorado Territory. The Carson forest had its headquarters in this dusty, few-street, many-cantina town, where ranching and realty ruled. The town squatted on a high desert plateau that was slung like a hammock between the Sangre de Cristo Mountains to the east and the San Juans to the west.

The Carson National Forest had been more heavily used—or abused—than the Apache. The last foresters had cheated away their jobs (until they were caught), allowing large cattle and sheep companies to graze their animals without limits. Massive gullies scissored across the landscape. "There is practically no game in this country," Aldo complained to his father. "Of course the sheep have run out all the deer; there are few turkeys, and I saw one place with bear-sign. Two elk were seen here two years ago."[18]

Leopold and his supervisor, Harry C. Hall, had been appointed by

University of Wisconsin-Madison Archives X25 1266

*Deputy Supervisor Leopold with six-shooters on his hips.*

Ringland to clean up the range—to cancel all illegal grazing permits, to chase out or take possession of illegal livestock, and to generally raise hell with the status quo. Harry Hall came into the job jangling his spurs and waving his rifle. Nobody misunderstood. He meant business.

Leopold took his place as Hall's right-hand man, the deputy supervisor, at $1,400 a year. The two set down strict new rules for running the forest. However, for the regulations to work, forest officers scattered over nine thousand square miles had to be kept informed. Headquarters was moved to Tres Piedras, which was closer to the forest's center (it was also thirty miles closer to Miss Bergere). A work crew strung the forest's first telephone wire between the office and the ranger stations, and in June 1911, the first issue of the *Carson Pine Cone* was put into the rangers' hands. The newsletter alerted the foresters to policy changes and provided conservation suggestions, tips for forestry efficiency, and good-natured ranger gossip. Leopold was listed as chief editor, illustrator, and contributor—the publication was probably his idea. The bannerhead read: "A Square Deal for Everybody, Special Favors for None."[19]

Throughout the reconstruction of Carson National Forest policies, Aldo showered Estella with mail. His first letters were polite, describing the daily occurrences of his life; the epistles evolved into intense, loving meanderings. Aldo spent a frustrating Fourth of July holiday in Santa Fe, during which Estella's "intended"—H. B. "Jamie" Jamison—stuck to her "like a leech."[20] Yet Estella gave Aldo some encouragement by shaking Jamison off. Shortly after, Aldo wrote his mother:

> It is *all up with me*. Five minutes after I saw Estella this time I could have told you what *I know* now—and that is I love her. . . . I have said nothing yet. But *somebody* is going to have to show their cards soon—and with Jamie on my mind I can't promise to wait any longer than my next chance.[21]

Aldo had a heavy workload, little money, and a lot of miles between himself and his new-found love. Jamie, on the other hand, was close by and rich, as well as being brilliant, handsome, and well-liked. As expected, Aldo did not hold Jamie in high esteem: "Jamie's soul is about like a

*The romantic triangle: Jamie, Estella, and Aldo are the three figures in the front. Luckily, Aldo had an ally in Arthur Ringland, now known affectionately as "Ring." In a letter to Marie on May 23, 1911, Aldo wrote: "Ring assures me he is going to be Jamie's little dog and stay right on deck all the time. Jamie will be consumed with wrath and indignation—and Ring will chuckle for a month."*[22]

silk-covered brick."[23] It had crossed Aldo's mind that Jamie could be after the Bergere family money and social connections. Few people in the Southwest came from a family as wealthy as Estella's or had ancestors as famous. Her father, Alfred M. Bergere, was a classical pianist and a rich, respected man in Santa Fe. Her mother, Eloisa Luna Otero Bergere, was descended from the Luna family, who traced their lineage back to Spanish royalty.

Long letters from Aldo were delivered to Estella as predictably as the sunrise, and she responded to them in a lighthearted way. Estella showed sincere appreciation when Aldo found a summer job at the Carson for her nineteen-year-old brother Luna. Otherwise, he received few hints of her feelings for him. Finally, he had to make a move. He packaged up his pin from the foresters' fraternity, the Society of Robin Hood, and sent it off to her. "In this little pin," he wrote, "is more than half my life."[24]

Estella stopped writing.

University of Wisconsin–Madison Archives X25 2949

*Aldo courting Estella on the tracks that connected them. On his return to Antonito, he wrote to her: "Today has been so endless that it seems as if ages had passed since we walked around by the Railroad tracks. Can one see the train from the schoolhouse at the place where it climbs into the hills a mile or so west of town? One can see the schoolhouse from there—I thought—but it was too far to see the White Peter and Thompson and the handkerchief—if they were there. But after all, I see them very plainly now—so what does it matter? Good night—and when you pass a lilac bush—pick a very little spray and wear it for me."*[25]

Leopold plunged into his work. Perhaps time would clear her head. Then on August 8, 1911, Chief Ringland came to inspect the Carson's new headquarters. He timed his visit so he could pass on the heavy news: Jamie had officially proposed.

Aldo sat up late that night thinking. He had to get to Santa Fe before Estella gave Jamie her answer. The next day, he pressed Hall for a short leave; his supervisor agreed, but the young deputy would have to wait two weeks.

Finally, on August 19, Aldo endured the slow burro back to Santa Fe. He spoke to Estella, but she demanded time to think. She had only met him four times, and most of what she knew of him was from letters.

University of Wisconsin-Madison Archives X25 1863

*Estella with some of her family, about 1907. Back row: Alfred Bergere (father), Eloisa Luna Otero Bergere (mother), Manuel Otero, Estella, and Nina Otero. Front row: Luna, Dolores, Rosina, and Consuelo.*[26]

Aldo took the long ride back to Tres Piedras.

While Estella examined her feelings, both families considered the situation. The Bergeres knew it would be difficult for a non-Catholic, German American to feel a part of their large southwestern clan. The Leopolds, too, could hardly imagine a Catholic, Spanish-Italian American melding into their family.

Everyone waited for Estella.

Aldo became more and more uneasy as weeks went on without an answer. He wrote to her, "A sort of restless discontent is gnawing at me. I am not exactly on the right side of my nerves."[27]

A month passed. Through the mail, Aldo heard that Estella was going with Jamie to the Montezuma Ball, Santa Fe's most important fall social event. Hall and Leopold had a supervisors' meeting in El Paso on November 10, not long after the ball was to take place. Aldo wrote Estella that he planned to stop in Santa Fe on the way to El Paso—to get his answer.

# New Life and Near Death
# 1912–1914

*After many days of much riding down*
*among thickets of detail and box canyons of routine,*
*it sometimes profits a man to top out [on] the high ridge*
*of leave without pay, and to take a look around. . . .*

*"To the Forest Officers of the Carson," July 15, 1913*[1]

Estella said yes.

After such news, Aldo could hardly concentrate. He wrote home, "Somehow, *this* time, I don't seem to be able to write."[2] On December 2, he wrote in his work journal, "In at least 6 lines of work today and nothing particularly accomplished in any one."[3]

Aldo celebrated the holidays and his engagement at the Bergeres' with his father beside him, warmly regaled with guitar music, Spanish and Italian carols, pasta, luminarias, and piñatas. Then came the promenade of New Year's fiestas and parties honoring New Mexico's statehood.

Work looked pretty dull in comparison. On his return to Tres Piedras, Leopold found his desk buried under requests for grazing permits. Altogether, Carson headquarters had received applications for 220,000 sheep. The new plan allowed only 198,000, and it was Leopold's job to reject the extra applications and to make the decisions stick. He and his rangers patrolled the forests, their six-shooters at their sides. Even so, they relied mostly on forceful words as a means of persuasion. When he met ranchers or sheepers to talk, Leopold carefully left his pistols in his saddle.

By March, the business of permits was well under way. Hall had accomplished the job he came for, and he moved on. Ringland promoted Leopold to acting supervisor of Carson National Forest. Aldo boasted to his fiancée: "Of all the men in our class from Forest School there are only two of us Acting Supervisors, and none are Supervisors yet."[4] By fall, he was Carson's full supervisor.

Leopold hired more rangers to hold the grazing situation steady. He closely inspected the rangers' stations, work journals, and reports. When a forester's idea or accomplishment impressed him, he dashed off "Bully!"[5] in the margin.

That summer, Aldo built a house for his bride-to-be, assisted by Estella's brother and his own brother Frederic, who was working at headquarters for the summer. Aldo's correspondence to his beloved never faltered.

> It has been such a happy playful spring-like day, as if some wild spirit were at play up there in the scudding clouds, flinging down madly whirling peltering little gusts of snow and then bursting suddenly into golden floods of sunshine. I love it all so, Darling, and I wished that *you* were here and that we could smile at that wild spirit up there *together*, darling.[6]

On October 9, 1912, Aldo and Estella married at the Cathedral of St. Francis in Santa Fe. Few events in Leopold's life, if any, proved as significant as this. Estella grew to be his closest companion, first adviser and editor, and the efficient and loving director of his home. She engendered all the joy, mischief, music, and laughter his more serious side neglected.

Aldo and Estella's honeymoon unfolded in their new little home that peered over the Rio Grande Valley. Without servants for the first time, Estella experimented in cooking, cutting hair, tramping through the woods, and hunting—even catching and skinning her own rabbits for dinner. During long, lamplit evenings, Aldo and Estella took turns reading to each other.

Bergere Collection, State Records Center & Archives, Santa Fe, NM

*The Leopolds on their wedding day with Estella's sister Dolores, and Carl, Jr. Younger brother Frederic said of Estella, "She was completely selfless, though she never made a show of it. She spoiled him—kept candy in his desk drawer—just as his mother had."*[7]

University of Wisconsin-Madison Archives X25 2931

*Aldo's drawing of a sunset at their Carson home, which he and Estella fondly called "Mia Casita," my little house. Aldo's parents sent a large load of furniture and household items to equip the new home.*

That spring, Leopold had to make some sheep arrangements in the western section of the forest, which was separated from the rest by the Jicarilla Apache Reservation. He placed his assistant, Ray Marsh, in charge of the office and prepared for the trip. Aldo was feeling a bit unwell, but nothing significant. Estella was pregnant, and she decided to visit her family in Santa Fe while he was away. The two of them set off by train, she riding south, and he heading northwest to Antonito and across the continental divide to Durango. From there, he hired a horse and rode south into the high Jicarilla Mountains.

Leopold touched base with the distant forest stations, settled disagreements, visited lambing sites, and lay down the law. Five days after his arrival, a hailstorm caught him in the mountains, soaking him in his bedroll. The skies doused him with rain, snow, and sleet for two days. The dampness seeped in.

As soon as he could, he rolled up his soggy bedroll and saddled up to ride east, hoping to run into rail lines where he might flag down a train. He got lost. An Apache man invited Leopold into his home to stay the night. A warm fire dried out his clothes, boots, and bones. The next day, Leopold mounted up, determined to make it home, but as he rode, his knees and legs grew so swollen he had to slash his boots. On April 21, he wrote in his work journal, "Very bad inflammation in knees, had to quit riding."[8]

Leopold finally made it to Chama, New Mexico, where he saw a doctor who diagnosed his illness as a bad case of rheumatism. It hardly sounded serious, so Leopold boarded the train for Tres Piedras. Once home, he didn't want to be disturbed by treatment. But when he staggered into the office on April 23, Ray Marsh was shocked. Aldo's face and limbs were so bloated he could hardly move. Marsh immediately insisted that Leopold take the train to Santa Fe to see a doctor. Aldo stubbornly replied that nothing was seriously wrong. He had just written to his father that he had had a "great trip" and was "exceptionally well but have a bad attack of rheumatism which amuses me greatly."[9]

He was wrong. In forty-eight hours, he would be near death. Marsh didn't know what the trouble was, but he knew it was severe. He got Leopold to Santa Fe.

Aldo's kidneys had failed; dangerous toxins were building up in his blood. The Santa Fe doctor ordered him to bed, piled him high with blankets, and gave him "sweating pills"[10] to clean the toxins out of his system and bring the swelling down. It worked, but barely, and very slowly.

The doctor correctly diagnosed Leopold's illness as Bright's disease, also called nephritis. Aldo was strictly confined to bed for six weeks. It was touch and go for many weeks. No one was sure how well his kidneys would recover, or what would happen if he suffered another attack. The doctor doubted Aldo could survive another one.

*Forest History Society, Durham, NC*

*Leopold's assistant, R. E. Marsh, was responsible for getting Aldo the medical attention that saved his life. This photo was taken in 1910 or 1911.*

Everyone heeded the doctor's warnings. Ringland visited, and granted Leopold paid sick leave without question. Afterward, Ringland reported to his assistant, "I hope his condition is not as serious as I am inclined to believe."[11]

During those first weeks, Leopold lay fairly still, struggling to gain weight and strength. "Getting stout," he wrote to Ring, "is really harder than getting well, it seems."[12]

After six weeks, Aldo was no more ready to ride a horse than to canoe the northern wilderness. Clara and Carl, Sr., begged him to come back to Iowa to recuperate. Ring gave him unpaid sick leave for a few months—until August 1913—and Aldo and Estella, who was five and a half months pregnant, carefully boarded the train to Burlington.

That summer, Aldo rested on the porch on Prospect Hill, smoking his pipe and staring out over the river, city, and bottomlands. His brush with death had convinced him that time might prove his enemy. He couldn't afford to put off his plans for protecting game species any longer.

In an article for the *Carson Pine Cone*, Leopold urged rangers to think about the overall health of the forest: "Letters, circulars, reports, and special cases beset our path as the logs, gullies, rocks, and bog-holes and mosquitoes beset us in the hills. We ride—but are we getting anywhere?"[13] He directed them to think independently, and to question forest policies that didn't protect the totality of the forest's resources, which he listed as "timber, water, forage, farm, recreative, game, fish, and 'scenic' resources."[14] Leopold's definition was more inclusive than that of the Forest Service policy, which was written, in his mind, only "to guide our daily task . . . it is not meant to confine our minds." He emphasized that all work should be valued according to "THE EFFECT ON THE FOREST."[15]

Writing for the *Pine Cone* was the closest Leopold would get to the Carson forest for awhile. He could not walk for a long stretch, and could only wonder what kind of job would be left for him in the Forest Service by the time he was able to return. He wrote to his fellow foresters, "The 'Rest Cure,' like greatness, is desired by some, while others have it thrust upon them. I wish I may soon be excused from the latter class."[16]

To keep himself busy, he read. He went back over many of his parents' books and magazines, and he purchased a copy of *Our Vanishing Wild*

*Life*, written by William Temple Hornaday, the director of the New York Zoological Society and founder of the Permanent Wild Life Protection Fund. (Aldo was so impressed, he gave the book to his father as a gift.) The book described in detail the plunging decline in wild species, especially game species, such as ducks, deer, and elk. After reading Hornaday's predictions, Aldo felt his mission to be all the more urgent. If something wasn't done soon, his children would never know the woods as he had. This point grew more important each day, as Estella grew larger and more eager to give birth.

On October 22, 1913, Aldo Starker Leopold entered the world, and there was much rejoicing, both in Burlington and Santa Fe.

In time during the child's naps, Leopold carefully built a plan for

University of Wisconsin-Madison Archives X25 2928

*Various scenes printed in the 1914* Carson Pine Cone, *wistfully drawn by Leopold as he looked on the life of a ranger from afar.*

University of Wisconsin–Madison Archives

*Estella and Aldo with Starker. Aldo wrote proudly, "Teddy Roosevelt is as placid as a mill pond before a rain, compared with that little Dickens."*[17]

turning some forest areas into game reserves. These reserves, he argued, could help save some game animals from extinction while making money for the Forest Service through the sale of hunting permits.

Leopold presented his game program in the January 1914 issue of the *Pine Cone*. The plan received mixed reviews—some rangers cheered, while others thought it just meant more work or extended the meaning of a forest too far. Traditionally, the individual states and territories had been responsible for protecting game; and though the system was ineffective, many rangers were unwilling to take up that role.

At this time, the Forest Service and the U.S. Bureau of Biological Survey (which evolved into the U.S. Fish and Wildlife Service) were agencies in their infancy, scrambling for turf and self-definition. Communication and cooperation between them were rarities. Articles in the *Pine Cone* proposed that the agencies work more closely together for game and fish conservation.

In February 1914, the doctor in Burlington allowed Aldo (then twenty-seven years old), Estella, and little Starker to return to the Southwest. The Leopolds soaked up sun, music, and the care of the Bergeres while Aldo waited for the day he could return to forestry. But the months passed, and so did much of Aldo's hope. He still tired too quickly.

In May, after one year of unpaid leave, the Forest Service laid Leopold off. Ring searched for a way to put him back onto the payroll, but nothing appropriate came up. Aldo just wasn't strong enough. In June, his doctor in Iowa called him back for further recovery time.

Aldo returned to the house on the bluff, while Estella and the little wild man stayed in Santa Fe. Aldo's visit was well timed: his father was suffering from prostate problems. The two of them sat on the porch and recovered together.

The more Aldo's body was forced to rest, the more his thoughts pushed and ran. His plans to save game animals in the national forests took deeper root. So did his meditations on the greater scope of life. His collection of notable quotations expanded widely over the summer. Ben Franklin made the grade with: "As we must account for every idle word, so we must account for every idle silence."[18] From Henry David Thoreau came (among other quotes): "In wildness is the preservation of the world."[19]

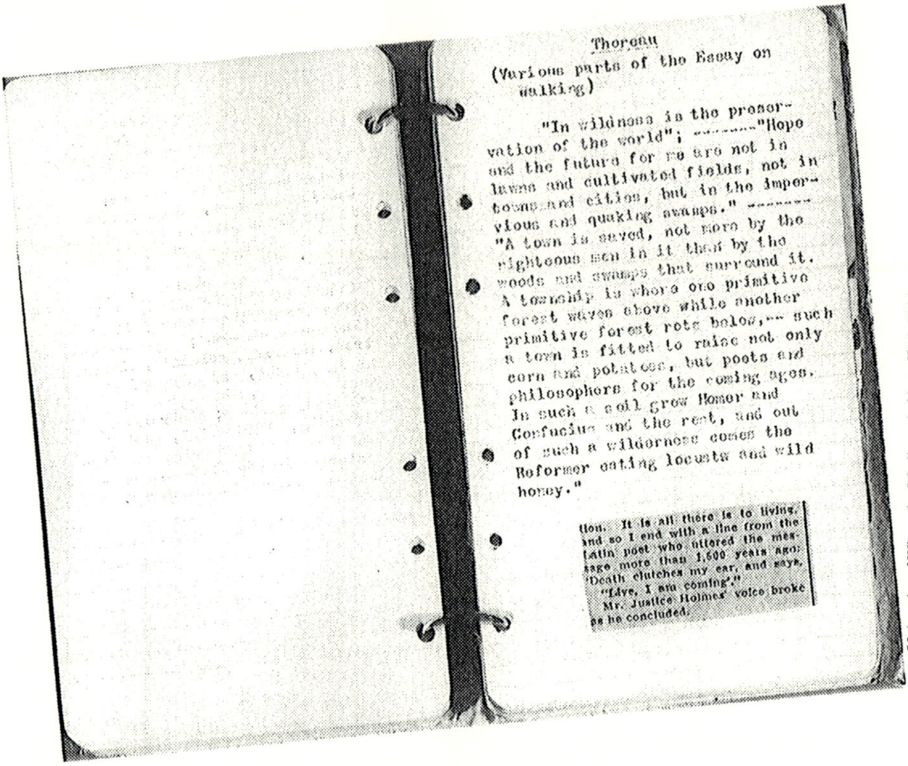


University of Wisconsin-Madison Archives X25 2930

*A page from Aldo's notebook of quotations. It encompassed the ideals he sought to emulate and attain: to fight mediocrity and hypocrisy, to increase enthusiasm and wisdom, to listen to others' opinions, to protect the natural world. Aldo recorded a wide range of voices, including those of John Muir, Miguel Cervantes, Henry Seidel Canby, Victor Hugo, John Stuart Mill, Epicurus, Cicero, John Milton, Voltaire, Theodore Roosevelt, Thomas Jefferson, Lao-Tzu, Ouspensky, the Bible, Edna St. Vincent Millay, Herodotus, Izaak Walton, Pai Ta-shin, Carl Sandburg, John Burroughs, Bertrand Russell, and Liberty Hyde Bailey.*

In late summer, Arthur Ringland came up with a position for Leopold in the district's Office of Grazing. It was only a desk job, true, but Aldo was grateful for anything at that point. He, Estella, and Starker moved into a small house in Albuquerque, not far from the Rio Grande.

Leopold reported for work in October 1914, after seventeen months away. He began the tedious job of pushing grazing permits, trespassing complaints, maps, budgets, and reports across his desk. Ring encouraged him to take time out to plan ways to build fires under the forestry workers who didn't "sweat much" about game protection. Unfortunately, Leopold would have to fight his way to the bottom of the pile first. At home, looking over at some ducks on the Rio Grande, Leopold mused to his father about his inability to even *hunt* game:

> Neither you nor I have worried the ducks much lately, have we? Doubtless they think you and I have grown to be a pair of good Hombres. I wish I could be on hand so we could *talk* ducks, anyhow, but so goes it.[20]

Late in November, Aldo's father went to Chicago for another surgery and returned to Burlington to recuperate. He took a turn for the worse, however, and on December 22, 1914, he died. Aldo took the first train back to Iowa.

The old year passed, and, for Aldo and Estella, so did remnants of childhood. They had each lost a parent (Estella's mother had died in September), and they had become parents themselves. In the world beyond them, violence encircled Europe, and war was tearing their ancestors' homelands apart.

Aldo's time of recovery ended. His turn to do something for the ducks had come.

# SAVE THAT GAME

# 1915-1919

*It is our task to educate the moral nature of*
*each and every one of New Mexico's half million citizens*
*to look upon our beneficial birds and animals,*
*not as so much gunfodder to satisfy*
*his instinctive love of killing,*
*but as irreplaceable works of art,*
*done in life by the Great Artist.*

*July 1917 speech to Albuquerque Rotarians*[1]

On January 15, 1915, a week after returning from his father's funeral and two days before his twenty-eighth birthday, Leopold handed in a memo on how to restore game in District 3. He proposed that Forest Service policy should:

- Consider game animals as forest "products" (just as trees are);
- Manage the wild species scientifically for count and quality;
- Set aside land for game refuges where hunting permits would be sold and limited;
- Use the profits to pay rangers to work on predator control and enforce state game laws.

A plan that covered these points, claimed Leopold, could successfully bring game back to the forests of the Southwest.

Ringland gave the memo his ardent approval. He recognized that, in essence, Leopold was asking the Forest Service to expand its definition of its responsibilities, and the proposal had importance for forests nationwide. Ringland advised Leopold to schedule a meeting with a representative from the Washington, D.C. office, Leon Kneipp.

Kneipp rejected Leopold's plan. The Forest Service would not sink any money into an expensive gamble. Kneipp felt that rangers should protect game out of a sense of public duty, and not expect any pay or time off from their tasks to do so. Nor would the Forest Service set aside land for game refuges until the public demanded it.

Needless to say, Leopold was disappointed. The rejection came at a time when he faced head on the shortsightedness of the Forest Service's policies in the grazing office. Leopold could see no way to encourage new seedlings without granting fewer grazing permits. His supervisor, John Kerr, cared only about revenues. He pushed Leopold to increase the number of permits, as well as to work out the forms and petty details. The two ended up in daily headlocks.

Frustration built up in Leopold like a mountain storm. Ringland hated to see one of his most innovative foresters wasted in paperwork. He knew he would lose Leopold if he didn't act quickly to find a position that suited Aldo's ambitions and abilities. Ring urged his friend to work on game-management ideas on the side while he tried to work out a better job for him.

Chafing at the bit, Aldo diverted his abundant creative energies to his home near the Rio Grande. He turned local timber into shelves, pieces of furniture, garden fences, and even a windmill. With exacting attention to detail, he carved and painted wooden duck decoys and made Christmas gifts. He took Starker on nature walks, studied Spanish with Estella, and experimented with different plant groupings in his garden. Though linnets harvested his lettuce and the chickens attacked the sunflowers for their seeds, Aldo persevered in good gardening humor. He wrote to his mother, "All of [this] is the struggle with nature, without which I should wilt like a transplanted cabbage."[2]

Aldo's happiness at home, however, did not dissolve his professional restlessness. Once again, Ringland came to the rescue. He created a new job just for Leopold—in public relations. Tourism was on the rise, and "recreation" was becoming a new forest product, especially in scenic areas.

He laid on Leopold's shoulders the responsibility for promoting recreation in the southwestern forests, while advising visitors how to take care of them. Leopold was also given Ringland's blessing to establish a fish-and-

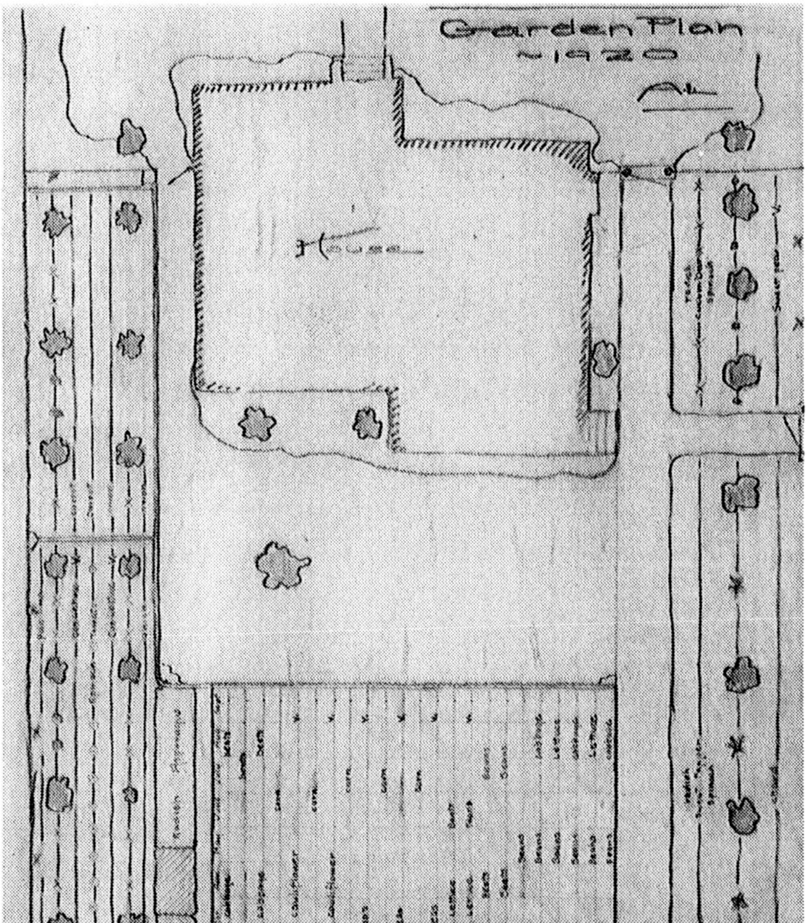


University of Wisconsin-Madison Archives X25 2938

*An example of the kind of garden plans Aldo made in Albuquerque. The Leopolds gardened for more than enjoyment. They depended on their harvests to stretch Aldo's salary of $1,800 a year. "We just stumble along over the cost of living from month to month," wrote Aldo to his mother. "However paid bills are more comfortable than new clothes."*[3]

game program to educate rangers on conservation practices.

The job was open and undefined. Leopold didn't trust it to last, but without a precedent to follow, he was finally free to put his creativity to use.

For five days in June of 1915, Leopold toured the Grand Canyon. He gazed down into the deep river gap that separated the yawning, multicolored cliffs. He inspected the trails, campgrounds, and other facilities on mule and horseback. The sights there were as distressing as they were awe-inspiring. Electric signs jutted out from the canyon rims. Store peddlers trumpeted their wares. Piles of uncollected garbage stained the trails and campsites. Untreated sewage ran into the river. The tourists had a death grip on the site.

Leopold and Forest Supervisor Don P. Johnston joined forces to halt the destruction. They had to construct a plan that would walk the tightrope between preservation and tourism, cracking down on inappropriate businesses and setting up zones to protect the canyon's most sensitive and scenic areas. Leopold and Johnston took Theodore Roosevelt's words on the canyon to heart: "Leave it as it is. You cannot improve on it; not a bit. The ages have been at work on it, and men can only mar it. . . . What you can do is keep it for your children and your children's children, and for all who come after you."[4] It would take two years to iron out the details and implement the Leopold/Johnston plan.[5]

When Leopold returned to his new office in Albuquerque, he badgered district rangers with questions about the numbers and kinds of animals, birds, and fish in their regions; he plied ranchers and farmers for the same information. After assembling his data, he wrote the first *Game and Fish Handbook* ever issued by the Forest Service. In it, Leopold set out to convince rangers of the economic and biological importance of every forest species—with the exception of predators. "The value of game," he wrote, "lies in its variety as well as its abundance."[6] Leopold provided rangers with descriptions of the many game species they might encounter, and surprisingly, he also included songbirds (Grandfather Starker would have approved). Leopold's plea for preserving species diversity (now known as biodiversity) was a first for the Forest Service.

The handbook, which came out in the fall of 1915, included methods

Grand Canyon National Park Museum (Fred Harvey Co.) 11813

Grand Canyon National Park Museum (Fred Harvey Co.) 11812

*The Grand Canyon Village in 1915, with tourist attractions extending along the rim. There were no adequate plans to limit development, ensure sanitation, or protect the land and wildlife in the face of a skyrocketing number of visitors.*

Department of Library Services, American Museum of Natural History 312378

*Dr. William T. Hornaday. Leopold deeply respected Hornaday's committed, albeit often wild-eyed, crusade to save the nation's wildlife from extinction.*

of stocking and feeding game to increase their numbers, and it outlined a system of forest game refuges. Leopold realized that his plan for game protection wouldn't have a chance if ordinary citizens didn't request and support it. There would be no refuges, no wardens, no laws, and no money to enforce the laws without pressure from hunters and anglers. So if he wanted to convert Leon Kneipp and the Forest Service, he would first have to change the public mind set.

Leopold began his own public relations campaign. He wrote letters and editorials, gave speeches, and published articles to convince local leaders and sporting groups that they needed game-protection societies.

The time was ripe. Game species had become so rare in places that hunters themselves were leading the conservation struggle. Back in 1911, a national organization had formed, sponsored by the Winchester Repeating Arms Company: the American Game Protective and Propagation Association (the AGPPA, which by 1913 had become the AGPA, or the American Game Protective Association). By 1915, the AGPA had enlisted numerous state groups to join the effort.

This was an opportunity to grasp quickly. Leopold believed that if average citizens from every state took command of the AGPA's leadership in their locality, the organization could be a tool for change. Otherwise, it would wither into a lobbying group for the gun and ammunitions manufacturers.

Leopold called for a citizens' group to represent New Mexico in the national organization. His industrious writing and speech making spawned action. Meetings were arranged with sporting groups and citizens in Albuquerque and Taos for October. The famous preservationist William Temple Hornaday agreed to attend one of Leopold's rallies. Ring watched with admiration from the sidelines at the hurricane he had unleashed.

Hornaday was touring the West, igniting a blaze of conservation concern. When he stood up in front of Leopold's group in Albuquerque, he showed slides of mutilated and dying deer, ducks, and other animals. The sixty-year-old man's voice shot out at the crowd, accusing, making predictions of extinctions and destruction, appealing, cajoling. Leopold watched this cranky, eccentric man brand the hearts of his listeners with a zeal for game protection. The sportsmen cheered, and Hornaday urged them to form the protection organization Leopold proposed.

In the quiet afterglow of the meeting, Hornaday gave Leopold an autographed copy of his newest book, *Wild Life Conservation in Theory and Practice.* "To Mr. Aldo Leopold, On the firing line in New Mexico and Arizona. With the kindest regards of the author."[7] It was a moment of great satisfaction for Aldo.

It came on the heels of the birth of his second son. Five days earlier, on October 8, 1915, Luna Bergere Leopold had arrived.

By the end of 1915, Albuquerque, Taos, Magdalena, and Santa Fe had all started game-protection societies. The Albuquerque branch elected Leopold secretary. In a summary of his Forest Service position for the Washington, D.C. office, Leopold listed some of the major successes of the societies:

> We have stocked more waters than ever before, including three heretofore empty ones. We have a complete census of the two threatened species; we have definite plans for saving them, and we have organized the forces to put these plans through. . . . We have forced both game wardens into unprecedented activity without losing their cooperation. Almost every issue of every important newspaper has something on game protection. A majority of Forest Officers have been converted from a passive or even apathetic attitude into activity and alertness.[8]

To keep the growing movement enthused, united, and informed, Leopold resurrected his old newsletter. The first issue of the renovated *Pine Cone* was delivered to members of the new game-protection societies and the district foresters in December 1915. Its stated goal was to "promote the protection and enjoyment of wild things" so that "every citizen may learn to hold the lives of harmless wild creatures as a public trust for human good."[9]

The inaugural issue covered a wide range of subjects: game laws and the Forest Service, the endangered Mexican mountain sheep, and Hornaday's first book. Leopold proposed that a national bird refuge be established at Stinking Lake, a shallow marsh on the Jicarilla Apache Indian Reservation, and he penned an essay on "The Varmint Question."

In it, he commented:

> It is well known that predatory animals are continuing to eat the cream off the stock grower's profits, and it hardly needs to be argued that, with our game supply as low as it is, a reduction in the predatory animal populations is bound to help the situation.[10]

Leopold called for all society members and foresters to work with sheepers and ranchers (the most vehement promoters of predator elimination) and the Biological Survey to reduce the number of "wolves, lions, coyotes, bob-cats, foxes, skunks, and other varmints."[11]

Over the next year, Leopold toured cities in southern New Mexico stirring up enthusiasm for conservation. The New Mexico Game Protective Association (NMGPA) was finally born; a thousand members strong, it chose Leopold as its secretary. It supported a federal bill, the Hornaday Plan, to establish a system of national wildlife refuges. The bill failed to pass, but the NMGPA members kept working for similar solutions.

Leopold traveled and continued to write, putting in many hours of overtime. His health, though, still hung in the balance. As much as he wanted to, he couldn't hunt. Estella did her best to protect him from worries at home. She took charge of the finances, worked out the budgets, tended the new baby, and meted out the discipline Starker often needed. Aldo adored her. No matter how important his work or his hobbies, he never became so involved as to take for granted or lose his connection with those he loved. He wrote love letters to Estella throughout his life whenever they were parted, and when they were together, they held hands both in public and private.

As Leopold was shifting to game-management work, the Forest Service was recognizing the trend and beginning to follow it. In Washington, D.C., a former professor of Leopold's from Yale, Henry Graves, had succeeded Gifford Pinchot. Leopold's initiative in data tracking and game-management efforts, and his talent for public relations, impressed Forester Graves. He directed Arthur Ringland to have Leopold transferred to the nation's capital to work on forest policies.

Leopold refused, pleading ill health. He wrote to Ringland, "I do not know whether I have twenty days or twenty years ahead of me. Whatever time I have, I wish to accomplish something definite. . . . This 'one thing' for me is obviously game protection."[12]

He was not, nor ever would be, a "company man"—not even for the Forest Service he loved. His independence, perfectionism, and idealism prevented him from taking or staying too long in any job that didn't fit his higher aspirations.

Besides, the Leopolds had firmly established their home in the Southwest. Aldo relished the fragrance of the wind, the view of the mountains, and the frontier style of living. He would often prop Starker up on the handlebars of his bicycle and pedal down to the Rio Grande to go fishing, one of his favorite pastimes.

Still, danger lingered. In the fall of 1916, Leopold suffered a relapse of nephritis. He took two weeks' rest and then relaxed his schedule. He stopped touring and finished writing his part of the Grand Canyon proposal.

When he turned thirty, in January 1917, Aldo could look back and feel confident that he had made great strides toward his "one thing." He had also begun establishing a name for himself in nationwide forestry journals, and he could paste into a scrapbook his first article printed in a popular magazine—*Arizona*. From this point on, Leopold never published fewer than two articles a year; often, his credits numbered more than a dozen.

A few days after his thirtieth birthday, Aldo received a letter from Theodore Roosevelt, an adviser for the AGPA:

> My dear Mr. Leopold,
> Through you, I wish to congratulate the Albuquerque Game Protective Association on what it is doing. I have just read the *Pine Cone*. I think your platform simply capital. . . . It seems your association in New Mexico is setting an example to the whole country.[13]

Then in July, Leopold and the NMGPA were recognized by—ironically—a preservationist group; William Temple Hornaday's

Permanent Wild Life[14] Protection Fund awarded them its Gold Medal. In his acceptance speech, Leopold explained the goal of the NMGPA: "to restore to every citizen his inalienable right to know and love the wild things of his native land."[15] He also introduced an idea that would reappear throughout his life in various transformations: that for conservation to become a reality, everyday people would have to change their moral and

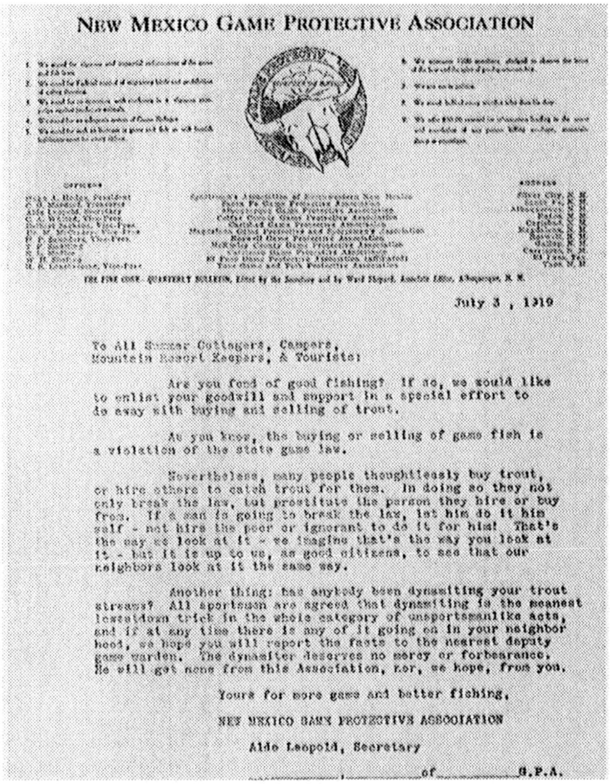

NEW MEXICO GAME PROTECTIVE ASSOCIATION

July 3, 1919

To All Summer Cottagers, Campers,
Mountain Resort Keepers, & Tourists:

Are you fond of good fishing? If so, we would like to enlist your goodwill and support in a special effort to do away with buying and selling of trout.

As you know, the buying or selling of game fish is a violation of the state game law.

Nevertheless, many people thoughtlessly buy trout, or hire others to catch trout for them. In doing so they not only break the law, but prostitute the person they hire or buy from. If a man is going to break the law, let him do it him self - not hire the poor or ignorant to do it for him! That's the way we look at it - we imagine that's the way you look at it - but it is up to us, as good citizens, to see that our neighbors look at it the same way.

Another thing: has anybody been dynamiting your trout streams? All sportsmen are agreed that dynamiting is the meanest lowestdown trick in the whole category of unsportsmanlike acts, and if at any time there is any of it going on in your neighbor hood, we hope you will report the facts to the nearest deputy game warden. The dynamiter deserves no mercy or forbearance. He will get none from this Association, nor, we hope, from you.

Yours for more game and better fishing,

NEW MEXICO GAME PROTECTIVE ASSOCIATION

Aldo Leopold, Secretary

_______, _______ of _______ G.P.A.

University of Wisconsin–Madison Archives X25 2942

*An example of one of the missives Leopold created as NMGPA Secretary. The official letterhead listed the organization's nine principles: "We stand for vigorous and impartial enforcement of game and fish laws. . . . for Federal control of migratory birds and prohibition of spring shooting. . . . for cooperation with stockmen in a vigorous campaign against predatory animals. . . . for an adequate supply of Game Refuges. . . . for such an increase in game and fish as will furnish legitimate sport for every citizen. We represent 1500 members, pledged to observe the letter of the law and the spirit of good sportsmanship. We are not in politics. We stand behind every warden who does his duty. We offer $50.00 reward for information leading to the arrest and conviction of any person killing antelope, mountain sheep or ptarmigan."*[16]

ethical outlook in regard to the natural world. The job of the NMGPA, he stated, was to "educate the moral nature of each and every one of New Mexico's half million citizens."[17] This was no small feat. "We have hitched our wagon to a star," Leopold admitted, "but we are using just ordinary axle grease to speed it on its stony way."[18]

The Aldo Leopold Foundation

*Estella hunting with Starker. She often accompanied her husband on his hunts. With her support, Aldo taught their children from an early age all the nuances of hunting safety and ethics, as well as the woodscraft that Carl, Sr., had taught him. Aldo wrote: "It is an honor to win by enterprise and skill the reputation of being a keen and successful sportsman. But to acquire a reputation for killing limits is a doubtful compliment, at best."*[19]

Following on these honors came a promotion, the first in four years. The Forest Service report read, "Mr. Leopold is a very brilliant man and an accomplished all-around Forest officer. He is considered one of the brainiest men in the District. . . . He is an indefatigable worker and largely interested in community welfare problems."[20]

The summer reached its summit for Aldo in August, with the birth of his first daughter, Adelina, who became known as Nina. His health had so improved by this time that he could tote the baby around and romp with the boys without worrying about a collapse. Slowly, and much to his delight, Aldo even began to hunt again.

In the spring of 1917, when the United States entered the European war that had been raging for three years, American concerns veered drastically from the course of conservation. The effort to defeat Germany drained people and supplies from the domestic front. Foresters volunteered for or were drafted into military service.

Leopold was passed over because of his health. He and other foresters who remained in the field were overworked during the day; in the evenings they were required to rally citizens to buy bonds and send their sons abroad. The army demanded more beef to feed the troops, so foresters were forced to multiply the grazing permits issued in the national forests. Like his colleague, Forester Elliot Barker, Leopold found staying with the Forest Service "pretty tough going."[21]

Late in 1917, the members of Albuquerque's Chamber of Commerce approached Leopold with a job offer. They had seen how quickly and effectively he had galvanized ordinary citizens into supporting game-protection societies and war-related civic projects, and they wanted him to do the same thing for their fair city. They tempted him with a substantial raise.

Since the war had annihilated government conservation, Leopold considered that now might be the time to concentrate on citizen activism. In January 1918, he resigned and went to work for the city of Albuquerque.

The city had a unique mixture of historical and cultural traditions, and Leopold urged citizens to take advantage of them—to capitalize on these differences rather than try to conform to the common mold of other cities. His new quarterly bulletin for the city, *Forward Albuquerque*,

A Chamber of Commerce is a Chamber of Citizenship. It's Primary Function Is to MAKE THE PUBLIC THINK

# Forward Albuquerque

QUARTERLY BULLETIN OF THE
Albuquerque, N. M. Chamber of Commerce

NO. 1. AUGUST, 1918

## SOME FACTS ABOUT RIO GRANDE PARK

## CITY PLANS AN ORNAMENT OR NECESSITY?

View of Volcanoes from Rio Grande Park

(Continued on Page 2).

*University of Wisconsin–Madison Archives X25 2941*

*A copy of Leopold's public relations tool for the city. He did for Albuquerque many of the same kinds of things his grandfather Starker had done for Burlington: he promoted the creation of parks, initiated city planning, fostered the arts, and encouraged citizen participation.*

proclaimed on its masthead: "A Chamber of Commerce is a Chamber of Citizenship. Its Primary Function Is to MAKE THE PUBLIC THINK."[22] He advised the city to hire a professional planner, to build in the style of the native Hispanic architecture, and to formalize a park along the Rio Grande. He also organized the city's Good Roads Bureau, which promoted road building and tourism, and he helped initiate a plan to drain the Rio Grande Valley for agriculture.

Leopold based his public relations and boosterism work on his own concept of "public spirit," which he defined as "year-around patriotism in action . . . intelligent unselfishness in practice."[23] He thought this spirit could be instilled through education—provide citizens with the facts, and they would make decisions based on enlightened self-interest. Once again dipping his toes into the pool of morality and ethics, he went so far as to postulate in a speech to the Albuquerque Women's Club, "Public-spirit is the new morality of the Twentieth Century."[24]

Public spirit, which for many was defined as patriotism, and its price were concerns that held many captive. Like a plague of locusts, the war could not be contained. Even the far reaches of the Southwest felt its appetite. Men, food, and forests were devoured by the war effort. Four hundred and twenty-seven war gardens were planted in Albuquerque. Estella's father, at sixty, went overseas with the Knights of Columbus to help wounded soldiers. Aldo's brother Frederic was assigned a fighting position on the French front in the Argonne Forest, where artillery fire had reduced the trees to stumps.

After months of intense fighting there, Frederic wrote, "Finally, the rumor of 'Armistice' spread." On November 11, 1918, "the firing ceased all at once in a great stillness."[25] A treaty had been arranged, and hope misted over a war-parched world.

In a letter written to his mother the next spring, Aldo wrote, "I come always to the same conclusion—that we live in a very happy island in a very sad world."[26] Two months later, the back page of the *Pine Cone* (which was still in Leopold's editorial hands) featured an article with these thoughts:

> The truth is, that in spite of all religion and philosophy, mankind

University of Wisconsin–Madison Archives X25 2950

*Luna, Starker, Estella, and Nina ready for the summer. As dedicated as Leopold was to his work, he reserved his evenings and weekends for his family.*

> has never acquired any real respect for the one thing in the Universe that is worth most to Mankind—namely Life. He has not even respect for himself, as witness the thousand wars in which he has jovially slain the earth's best. Still less has he any respect for other species of animals. . . . The trouble is that man's intellect has developed much faster than his morals.[27]

As the world struggled to recover from the war, the Forest Service scrambled to regain its footing. Chief Forester Henry Graves wanted Leopold back. It would take time, however, to prepare the right position for him. Leopold, though, was examining the possibility of a position with the AGPA. He was tiring of the Good Roads Movement and city boosterism—the unholy alliances he observed between business interests, advertising, and designated civic projects and movements. Furthermore, he was becoming disenchanted with the chamber's role as a leader of business—many of the business people seemed unable to think and act independently or grasp values beyond those of short-term economics.

Waiting for new job opportunities to materialize, Aldo bought his first automobile, a Ford. As Estella and the children packed for a train trip to visit California relatives, Aldo assembled his tackle for a fishing trip with his brother Carl. "I'm tickled as a small boy to be off,"[28] he wrote.

He put his new car in gear, and the brothers were on their way.

# A Wild Proposal
## 1919-1924

*Wilderness is a resource which can shrink*
*but cannot grow.*

*"Defenders of Wilderness,"* A Sand County Almanac

On August 1, 1919, Aldo was appointed to the second-highest position in District 3—Assistant Forester in Charge of Operations. Numerous foresters grumbled that Leopold didn't deserve the job and was hardly suited to its enormous responsibilities. He hadn't proven he was versed enough in all aspects of forestry management to handle the overarching tasks of inspecting every forest, reporting on what he found, and suggesting improvements.

Leopold had a rigorous schedule to follow—three forests per summer, with a month at each. Since the Forest Service had no set inspection method, Leopold had to develop his own. His first reports were sketchy. He wrote more comments on rangers' initiative and reading habits than on the details of their work or the conditions of their fire stations.

During a late-summer tour of his old stomping ground, the Carson, Leopold roved further south into the Datil Forest. He fished away a Sunday at the headwaters of the Gila River and came away relaxed and refreshed. No telephone poles or roads cut across the landscape; there were just the pines, the trout, the tingle of fresh, pungent air, and a breeze alive with bird calls.

Few areas like this remained in District 3. Was there, he wondered, a legal way to preserve the canyonlands around the Gila just as they were?

That December, at a meeting of district foresters in Salt Lake City, Leopold heard about a young forest assistant named Arthur Carhart from District 2 in Colorado. Carhart, the Forest Service's first landscape architect, had been dubbed the "Beauty Engineer"[1] by his co-workers. Carhart had recommended that Trappers Lake, in the White River National Forest, be permanently preserved in a wilderness state—no so-called improvements. On his return trip, Leopold stopped by the D-2 offices to meet the man.

Forest History Society, Durham, NC

*Trappers Lake: view from the west shore in 1916. To those who argued that the earth was made to be developed and used, Leopold responded: "God started his show a good many million years before he had any men for an audience—a sad waste of both actors and music. . . . it is just barely possible that God himself likes to hear birds sing and see flowers grow."*[2]

Up to this point, attempts to set aside natural areas in the national forests led only to national parks or "primitive areas" that were open to later development. Leopold did not trust the park system to preserve any wilderness area intact. It had a reputation for poor management with a lax attitude toward protection. The goal of the park system seemed to be to build as many roads to scenic areas and shuttle as many tourists through the system as possible. "To cherish we must see and fondle," Aldo wrote in discouragement about tourism, "and when enough have seen and fondled, there is no wilderness left to cherish."[3]

Officially preserving a forest in its natural state sawed against the

*Forest History Society, Durham, NC*

*Forester Arthur Carhart in the Superior National Forest of Minnesota in 1920. In his memo on the meeting with Leopold, Carhart wrote: "There are portions of natural scenic beauty which are God-made, and the beauties of which of a right should be the property of all people . . . not only of the Nation, but of the world."*[4]

grain of Pinchot's "wise-use" approach. Leopold and Carhart realized that they faced an enormous philosophical log jam ahead of them. Carhart organized his arguments for preservation from a scenic and aesthetic approach, while Leopold took the stand for recreation—preserving the wilderness adventure. The meeting of these two foresters, both driven by the need to preserve a limited treasure, marked the beginning of a struggle to change the Forest Service's view of natural areas.

Leopold returned to Albuquerque invigorated by his new cause. But Frank C. W. Pooler, the new Chief Forester of District 3, was less than enthused with his assistant. He had heard complaints about Leopold from rangers in the field: the new man was neither tactful nor thorough enough.

Pooler offered Leopold a transfer to the northern Rocky Mountains: he could be chief of operations in District 1. Leopold declined. He loved the Southwest, and he didn't want to leave his game-protection and wilderness projects unfinished. Nor did he want to move his family. Estella was even more bound to the Southwest, by love, tradition, and family, and the couple was expecting their fourth child. Aldo Carl Leopold was born within weeks, on December 18, 1919.

Pooler did not push him further, but he reported to Forester Henry Graves in Washington, D.C.:

> I consider him a Chief of Operations *in the making*. . . . There is an extraordinary amount of ability and originality stored up in this man. The FS can hardly afford to lose it. It will be my business to try to draw it out and get it properly applied, just as it will be his business (and I have told him so in so many words) to win my confidence as an operations man.[5]

Leopold took up Pooler's challenge. He withdrew slightly from the NMGPA, which was directing its conservation efforts with less and less prompting. He edited the last regular issue of the *Pine Cone* in 1920, and at the 1920 American Game Conference in Washington, D.C., he was able to wind up his NMGPA commitment with a triumphant report describing how a Game and Fish Commission had been established in the state, along with a system of bird and game refuges (based on his own plan). His news on predator control was as impressive: less than three years earlier, three hundred wolves had roamed New Mexico; by the time of the report, only about thirty remained and but a few mountain lions.

Having attained many of his goals for NMGPA, Leopold was able to throw his energies completely into his new role, examining each forest with the intensity of a scientist. The closer Leopold looked, the more he saw that made him uneasy. Overgrazing and poor logging practices had stripped the forests of their protective layers of grasses, ground cover, and saplings. Long, hideous gashes cut across hillsides where water had dragged off the topsoil or wind had scoured it away. Leopold wrote to his mother: "One day, we came home with cakes of mud a quarter of an inch thick surrounding our eyes—stuff that had blown into our eyes and 'teared' out so you had to pull off the lumps every few minutes."[6]

*Arizona Historical Society, Tucson (William C. Barnes Collection)*

*In his forest inspections, Leopold observed gullies such as these photographed in 1910 in the Coconino National Forest of Arizona, caused by the heavy grazing of sheep.*

The evidence was overwhelming. Ninety percent of the topsoil had been washed off the land along the Blue River in the Apache National Forest, the area that had been so beautifully wild in Leopold's early foresting days. Twenty-seven of the thirty forests he examined during his time as chief of operations were severely impaired or destroyed by erosion.

Leopold researched the topic and consulted with experts, often with the man he would come to think of as the erosion "prophet,"[7] Charles Cooperrider. Leopold concluded that merely calling a halt to overgrazing would not cure the topsoil runoff or heal the gashes in the earth. Foresters would have to work to restore what had been lost. They would use such techniques as building rock dams in ditches and stone ledges on hillsides, and planting willows along streams to restore the rangeland and check the loss of soil. He also theorized that some arid areas should never be grazed; the continual chewing of plant shoots and pounding of hooves on the shallow roots could turn delicate areas to desert.

Shortly after his thirty-fourth birthday, Leopold summed up the conclusion of his research in a speech at the University of Arizona: soil "is the basic natural resource."

> Destruction of the soil is the most fundamental kind of economic loss which the human race can suffer. With enough time and money, a neglected farm can be put back on its feet—if the soil is there. By expensive replanting and with a generation or two of waiting, a ruined forest can again be made productive—if the soil is there. . . . But if the soil is gone, the loss is absolute and irrevocable.

He also emphasized that many devastating natural phenomena were not acts of God, but were the results of causes and effects that could be traced to human decisions.[8]

Leopold's erosion inspections and "loyal assistance"[9] finally attained Frank Pooler's confidence. The Forest Service, however, now had a new director—William B. Greeley. Greeley was not satisfied with the state of District 3 forests or with Leopold's reports. In his opinion, Leopold focused too much on the land and not enough on the mechanics of forestry: tools, fire stations, and cost accounting. Greeley strongly suggested that Leopold accept a transfer to the Forest Products Laboratory in Madison, Wisconsin. Since Leopold had an inquisitive nature, a background in research, and a real interest in forest conservation, Greeley believed he could lead the laboratory in discovering new ways to save trees and develop timber wastes into useful products.

Leopold declined. Life was good. He was back in the Forest Service doing work he believed in, and prospects for promotion looked good. Physically, he felt better than he had in several years, and he and the older boys had joined the Tome Hunt Club near Albuquerque. They all enjoyed hunting there so much that there always arose a competition between Starker and Luna about who should go along if only one could go. They had to draw straws to settle the issue. Much later, Starker recalled, "If I won, fine. If Luna won, then I would trade him out of it with one thing or another. Every damn thing I had except my pocket knife."[10]

Greeley remained unconvinced of the wisdom of Leopold's decision to stay put, but he accepted it for the present on the condition that things around District 3 start to meet his standards. Major Evan Kelley was sent down to observe and advise Leopold on his 1921 spring tours of the Apache and Sitgreaves national forests, and to help with the inspections. As the two men traveled over trails by day and set up camp by sunset's waning light, they discussed the goals of inspection and how these aims should be achieved. Though Kelley liked Leopold's "absence of satisfaction with the what-is's of the time and his restlessness of mind,"[11] he found him too sure of his own opinions, and too careless. Leopold didn't pay enough attention to details. His head was too high in the clouds, and his feet were "somewhat off the ground."[12]

After Kelley's visit, Leopold covered a greater range of elements in his inspection reports, organized them more clearly, and packed them with details. Leopold invented a system of tally sheets that encompassed the myriad categories and minute details that had to be checked—even down to the outhouses. His system was eventually adopted for use by the entire Forest Service. Later, Leopold wrote to Kelley, "I thought I knew how to work before you showed up in District 3, but . . . I was just playing with my job until you demonstrated how to heave with both shoulders, and especially how to steady the heaving process to make it more effective."[13]

Eventually, Leopold's hard work, tireless energy, passion for testing theories, and "splendid imagination"[14] proved to nearly all the district's foresters that he could handle his job.

As engrossed as he was in his work on erosion and in gaining Chief Greeley's confidence, Leopold continued to struggle for the preservation of natural areas. He supported Carhart's Trappers Lake proposal, helping him save the shoreline of the lake from tourist cabins and roads. When Carhart went on to map out a plan that would safeguard hundreds of wild, granite-lined, pine-rimmed lakes in the Superior National Forest of northern Minnesota (the boundary waters between the state and Ontario), Leopold followed him with as much political and public leverage as he could inspire.

Leopold's larger goal, however, was to diminish the Forest Service's resistance to such proposals. In a 1921 article published in the *Journal of Forestry*, Leopold recommended that the Service once again expand its definition of itself—beyond producing timber and protecting game to protecting wilderness as a recreation resource. He defined wilderness as a "continuous stretch of country preserved in its natural state, open to lawful hunting and fishing, big enough to absorb a two weeks' pack trip, and kept devoid of roads, artificial trails, cottages, or other works of man."[15] (In contexts broader than the Southwest, he added canoe trips to the list of recreations.)

Leopold argued for the preservation of wilderness on the grounds that the "highest use" was not always an industrial or commercial use, especially when the public was calling out for the chance to experience places devoid of development. If people wanted to get "back to nature," he wrote, the government ought to preserve "a little nature to get back to."[16] And, if the Forest Service was to serve the needs of the entire public—not just the majority—a variety of recreational experiences ought to be made available within the preserved lands. Leopold capped his argument with a proposal to set aside the high box-canyon reaches of the Gila Forest as wilderness. The area exemplified the unique mountain regions of the Southwest, and it was the only area of its kind remaining undeveloped in the forest system. "It will be much easier and cheaper to preserve, by forethought . . . than to create it after it is gone."[17]

Within the year, Chief of Operations Leopold had the 750,000 acres around the headwaters of the Gila in the Mogollon Mountains surveyed.

In his report to Frank Pooler, he recommended that no additional grazing permits be given, and that no homes, businesses, or other superfluous buildings be allowed in the area. Trails, phone lines, and fire stations could remain, but the wilderness designation would cut a moat of protection around the unimproved area.

Pooler was impressed. The report on the Gila Forest as a whole, and the wilderness proposal in particular, exemplified the "painstaking detail" and "comprehensive work"[18] Leopold was accomplishing.

By the fall of 1922, Leopold was long overdue for a vacation out in some wild, untamed place. Aldo and his brother Carl (now also his brother-in-law, having married Estella's sister Dolores in July 1921) ventured down into Mexico, into the swampy back regions where the Colorado River emptied into the Gulf of California—a wilderness in the truest sense. Aldo wrote in his journal of the green lagoons he found there (later revised into an essay):

> The still waters were of a deep emerald hue. . . . At each bend we saw egrets standing in the pools ahead, each white statue matched by its white reflection. Fleets of cormorants drove their black prows in quest of skittering mullets. . . . Often we came upon a bobcat, flattened to some half-immersed driftwood log, paw poised for mullet. Families of raccoons waded the shallows, munching water beetles. Coyotes watched us from inland knolls. . . . At every shallow ford were tracks of burro deer.[19]

This was a healthy land—the plants were lush, the animals active and undisturbed, the soil held firmly in place. The body of the land pulsed with life, all its organs functioning smoothly.

With the wild Mexican forests for comparison, the lands of District 3 seemed tame and in even greater peril. The more minutely Leopold inspected his forests, the more complex the relationship he discovered between a forest's erosion crisis and its flora and fauna. Far more disturbing, Leopold realized that few in the Forest Service knew more than he did. He feared the increasing consequences of policies that were being made without scientific information, for they were proving more harmful than helpful.

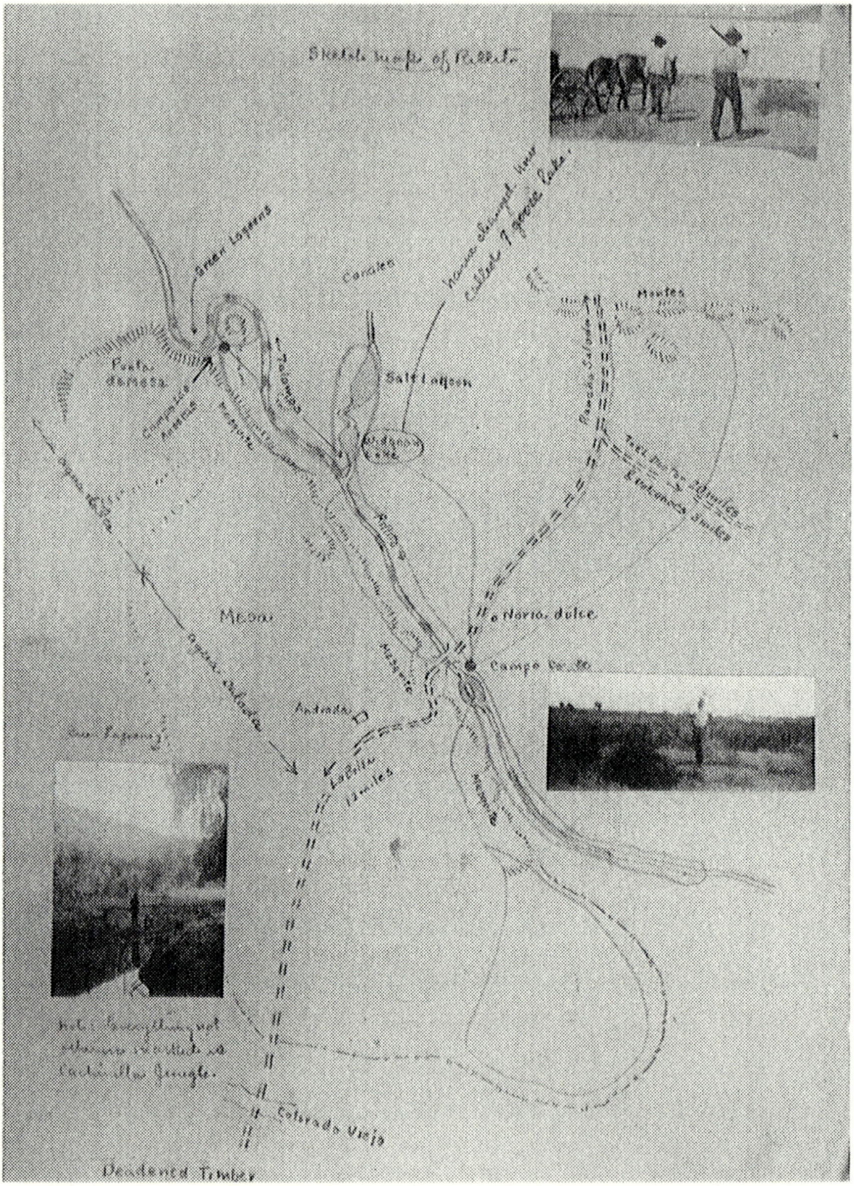


University of Wisconsin–Madison Archives X25 1857

*A page from the hunting journal Leopold kept on his trip to the Colorado River Delta in Mexico. Much later in life, he heard that the land had been turned into farms for growing melons. He wrote: "Man always kills the things he loves, and so we pioneers have killed our wilderness. Some say we had to. Be that as it may, I am glad I shall never have to be young without wild country to be young in."*[20]

Leopold mapped the damage in each forest and examined fire scars to uncover its fire history. He used this to create a mosaic of interrelated histories—climate, plant, animal, and cultural—against the backdrop of erosion. Then he wrote the first Forest Service manual on erosion control—the *Watershed Handbook*, published in 1923. (Leopold saw it as "the first section of the proposed 'Lands Handbook,' which will extend and supersede the present 'Uses Handbook.'"[21]) The *Watershed Handbook* explained the importance of watersheds, the nature of erosion in the Southwest, and the causes of erosion and relating factors; it detailed natural and artificial erosion controls, including plants that could control erosion; it listed problems and remedies; and it suggested organizations that might be able to work cooperatively on the erosion control effort. Leopold's handbook was so comprehensive that it became a catalyst in the Forest Service's evolving view of and approach to watersheds and erosion.

Leopold saved the rest of his research for another pet project—a thorough historical study of the Southwest's lands and wildlife, called "Southwestern Game Fields." Two friends with long-standing interests in game and hunting, J. Stokley Lignon and R. Fred Pettit, agreed to help him collect additional information, analyze the data, and write up the results.

Over the ensuing months of inspections and ongoing research, Leopold became convinced that range grasses held the soil in place better than underbrush, even though the existing Forest Service fire-prevention policy promoted grazing to keep grasses down. Leopold's 1923 essay, "Some Fundamentals of Conservation in the Southwest," shot holes in the Forest Service logic:

> All our existing knowledge in forestry indicates very strongly that overgrazing has done far more damage to the Southwest than fires or cuttings. . . . A century of fires without grazing did not spoil the Sapello [a stream in the Gila National Forest], but a decade of grazing without fires ruined it.[22]

As in earlier and later essays, Leopold hinted that fire, "the scourge of all living things,"[23] was not always a forest's worst enemy. In fact, he posited, fire might be a necessary ingredient in the growth of some forest species.[24] Leopold went on to caution that the language of dollars and cents could never adequately direct Forest Service policies or citizens' attitudes toward the land. "The privilege of possessing the earth," he wrote, "entails the responsibility of passing it on, the better for our use, not only to immediate posterity, but to the Unknown Future."[25]

Influenced by the Russian philosopher Piotr D. Ouspensky, Leopold imagined the land as a living being "vastly less alive than ourselves in degree, but vastly greater than ourselves in time and space—a being that was old when the morning stars sang together, and, when the last of us has been gathered into his fathers, will still be young."[26]

Though he sent this essay around to his colleagues for comments, Leopold chose not to publish it. Neither the Forest Service nor the nation were taking time to ponder the issues Leopold was considering. The postwar years were marked by a new, feverish prosperity, and citizens across America were taking their vacations to travel. Advancing the Good Roads Movement, the government built thoroughfares through every scenic area it could identify.

Leopold, Carhart, and others protested. (Leopold later wrote: "Recreational development is a job not of building roads into lovely country, but of building receptivity into the still unlovely mind."[27]) In March 1923, Leopold made his first public presentation of his Gila wilderness proposal and his policy plan for natural areas in the national forests. He addressed other district foresters at a meeting in Utah and asked for their votes of approval. That night he wrote home:

> Stella Dearest . . . I feel pretty blue this afternoon, because I'm pretty sure to be voted down on my Wilderness Policy—although everybody commended my speech. But I guess I must stick to my crazy ideas in spite of turn downs. I'll pull [the plan] through yet.[28]

Leopold's proposal failed, but his articles in popular magazines on the necessity of wilderness for history and adventure drew national attention. Many cheered from the sidelines, but critics called him "anti-road" and said his plan for "locking up resources" was wasteful. Others protested that wilderness areas would end up as playgrounds for the rich.

Leopold responded that the desire for intermittent escapes to "uncivilized" stretches of land was embedded deep in the American psyche. The only way to provide democratic access to these lands would be to protect roadless, wild places in the name of the public and future generations. He wrote: "What degrees of wilderness, then, are we discussing? The answer is *all* degrees. Wilderness is a relative condition. . . . It is just as unwise to devote 100 percent of the recreational resources of our public parks and forests to motorists as it would be to devote 100 percent of our city parks to merry-go-rounds."[29]

The public debate over "the wilderness idea" had begun.

Other foresters and conservationists such as Evan Kelley, Frederick Winn, Ernest Oberholzer, and Robert Marshall, heard Leopold's call for action and responded with cheers of support. Forester and friend Frank Waugh said: "When Leopold's trumpet call rang through the forest, echoes came back from every quarter. Thousands of foresters and hundreds of common nature lovers felt the same way about it."[30]

Leopold's unique work in wilderness protection, erosion control, and game management garnered attention from many corners. Chief William Greeley again insisted that Leopold transfer to the Forest Products Laboratory in Madison; the lab needed a man of Leopold's talents and stature. The present director was expected to resign within the year, and Greeley pressed Leopold to take the temporary job of assistant until he could take over the directorship.

Leopold was primed to move from observation to scientific experimentation; perhaps he saw this as the opportunity he needed. Or perhaps Greeley simply pushed him hard enough. Whatever the reason, Leopold finally gave in.

The Forest Products Laboratory was a thousand miles from the place the Leopolds called home. Family and friends were stunned. District 3 mourned its loss. Members of the Albuquerque Game Protective Association could not imagine the organization without Leopold. They threw him a going-away party: more than a hundred people sent him off with good wishes, a pocket watch, and a new shotgun.

On May 29, 1924, Leopold left for Wisconsin. Five days later, Frank Pooler approved his Recreational Working Plan for the Gila Wilderness Area—the first official wilderness area in a national forest.

# Surveying the Field

# 1924-1933

*A game manager must acquire the scientific point of view. . . .*
*Facts about game must be found before they can be taught.*

Game Management[1]

Since Assistant Director Leopold was not needed at the lab until July 1, he took the train with Starker and Luna to Burlington to visit his mother and brothers. (Marie had married and moved to Illinois with her husband.) Together again, the "boys" immediately began plans for a trip—this time to Carhart's proposed wilderness area in the boundary waters of Minnesota for two weeks of canoeing, camping, and fishing.

Prior to trip departure, though, Aldo had to travel to Madison to prepare the way for the family move. Starker and his uncles Carl and Frederic headed straight to Ely, Minnesota, to arrange for the canoes and equipment (Luna stayed with Opa Leopold to await the arrival of the rest of his family).

Their missions accomplished, Aldo and the other adventurers met and set off into the wilds of the Superior National Forest and the Canadian Quetico. The Leopold brothers had at last reached their magical North. For two weeks, the voyageurs paddled past granite outcroppings and tall pines, fishing for trout and listening to the mournful wail of loons. Aldo wrote in his journal, "The number of adventures awaiting us in this blessed country seems without end."[2] Later he added, "How Dad would have

*Clara Starker Leopold. Aldo remained close to his mother all his life, keeping up a regular, though no longer daily, correspondence with her. As a youth, he had written to her: "Never, in any age, at any time, in any land, has a man been given as many chances to make good in life as* I *have been given, and let me also say with Abraham Lincoln, . . . 'All that I am, or hope to be, I owe to my angel mother.'"*[3] *University of Wisconsin-Madison Archives X25 1086*

loved it! I am reminded of Isaac [sic] Walton's terse but loving tribute—'an excellent angler, now with God.'"[4]

Leopold and Starker returned to Madison, an "awfully dolled up town."[5] He had written earlier to Estella: "Nobody has any backyard except in the slums—not even a woodshed or fence or chickens—the backyards are open lawns just as the fronts. We have a little garden room at this place I am thinking of—which is not usually the case, but *nobody* keeps chickens, so we would do so at our own peril!"[6] The rest of the family arrived shortly, and the Leopolds moved into a rented home "not far from the country."[7] Within the month, they bought a stucco house about a mile from the lab—at 2222 Van Hise Avenue—and their energies went into transforming it into a real home. They planted gardens and put up birdhouses and feeders. Brokenhearted over the move, Estella gardened her way out of the doldrums.

*University of Wisconsin–Madison Archives X25 1267*

*Aldo in 1924 with his catch from northern waters. "Watching the grey twilight settling upon our lake, [we] could truly say that 'all our ways are pleasantness and all our paths are peace.'"*[8]

*The Leopold home at 2222 Van Hise Avenue. The street was an appropriate place for Aldo: Charles Van Hise, once president of the University of Wisconsin at Madison, had written one of the classics of the early environmental movement:* The Conservation of Natural Resources.

Though Aldo adapted to his new urban surroundings, he never quite adjusted to the workings of the laboratory. Acrid glues and testing machines would never call to him like wind rustling fallen leaves or sunlight dappling the forest floor. Nor did Director Winslow ever resign. For four years, Leopold remained "a tie pickler" and "timber-tester"[9] (a profession—that of industrial scientist—that he had disparaged as a student). Though committed to the conservation principles embedded in the concept of extracting the greatest use out of the timber forested, he was not interested in the chemical and manufacturing processes that were involved. He did, though, excel at the public relations tasks: he strengthened the cooperation between foresters and the laboratory; he encouraged the public to reduce waste and increase their use of lower grade woods and alternative wood products. And he did gain a thorough knowledge of the techniques of laboratory science. But the study of commercial products repelled him; he longed to apply the scientific methods he was learning to advance his understanding of the land and its workings.

Fortunately, mill and forest inspections allowed him to escape the

University of Wisconsin-Madison Archives X25 1071

*Aldo Leopold, assistant director of the USDA Forest Products Laboratory in Madison. A coworker called him "a fish out of water. . . . We were scientists, engineers; Leopold was a forester."*[10]

laboratory often enough to preserve his sanity. One western survey took Leopold and his associates to California. He wrote to Estella of the panoramic views that greeted him: "We went through the Sierras for two days. If the Lord ever made another country like that, it wasn't on this particular star."[11] His enchantment with the beauty of the scenery, however, was counterweighted by his disenchantment with the mind set of the typical American tourist.

> I can't say whether it was more pleasure to see Yosemite than pain to see the way most people see it. It's a struggle for me sometimes to play ball with the crowd at all. How much compromise is a question on which there is no such thing as advice or consolation. Every man is a lone wolf when he faces real realities. . . . The tourists all gape at Yosemite but what none of them see is the fifty miles of foothills on the way in. [The hills] are almost a relief after the highly frosted wedding cake (and the wedding guests) on the other end.[12]

Leopold was beginning to pay the price of being a visionary. He had to fight to keep his ego in check and his quest intact. He later wrote: "One of the penalties of an ecological education is that one lives alone in a world of wounds. Much of the damage inflicted on the land is quite invisible to laymen . . . in a community that believes itself well and does not want to be told otherwise."[13]

Frustrated by his work and forced to neglect his vision, yet with more free time than before, Aldo threw his energies into various conservation and leisure clubs, including the Get-Away Club, the Kumlien Club (an ornithological study group), and the Izaak Walton League of Wisconsin. Under his direction, the league backed the formation of the Boundary Waters Canoe Area, raising the furor of the national wilderness debate.

Aldo relaxed by pursuing "adventure," which he considered, along with sunshine, air, food, work, and love, as one of the "necessaries" of life. Leopold once counseled a group of university students not to waste their leisure time doing what everyone else did:

> It is because the vast majority of people do not have the courage to venture off the beaten path that they fail to find [adventure], and live lop-sided lives. . . . A good healthy curiosity is better equipment to venture forth than any amount of learning or education. . . . The beaten paths of conformity are literally a prison.[14]

He added, "I confess my own leisure to be spent entirely in search of adventure without regard to prudence, profit, self-improvement, learning, or any other serious thing."[15]

In 1926, Aldo read the recently published *Hunting with the Bow and Arrow* by Saxton Pope. Bow hunting struck him as a purer form of sport than gun hunting, because it required more skill and resulted in less killing. Thus, archery fever infected him. ("You do not annex a hobby, the hobby annexes you."[16]) He, Estella, and the older children slung quivers over their shoulders and began target practice in the park along Lake Wingra or in the country. To increase the challenge (and adventure) they practiced doing roving shoots, where they picked targets on the move. The whole family took to the sport. Estella became so skilled she won the Wisconsin women's championship five years running and took fourth at nationals.

University of Wisconsin-Madison Archives X25 1038

*Estella Leopold with Starker, Ginny Emlin, Aldo, and John Emlin about 1940. After the state and national tournaments, the newspapers dubbed Estella "The Diana of the Hunt."[17] She joined the faculty of the University of Wisconsin at Madison to teach archery.*

A good hobby in modern times, as Leopold defined it, was one "that entails either making something or making tools to make it with, and then using it to accomplish some needless thing."[18] Though he never matched his wife's mastery of the sport, he became a master at fashioning his own archery tackle. Starting with a fine stave of yew a friend at the lab

*Aldo and his daughter Estella in front of the house in 1927. A devoted family man, Leopold asked his children each night at dinner, "What did you do that was interesting today?" Nina confessed that she often spent much of the day trying to come up with something worthwhile to tell him.*[19]

gave him, he experimented with an array of glues, varnishes, animal horns, and imported woods in his basement workshop. Estella often brought her knitting down and sat with Aldo while he worked on his bows and arrows. (The entire family eventually made their own tackle.) Luna remembered one yew bow of his father's "that had a flatter trajectory than any of us had ever seen before or since. It shot point blank at 100 yards. Boy, that was a piece of equipment."[20]

Archery tackle was not the only thing the Leopolds crafted. They still valued homemade Christmas gifts over store-bought ones, and the children experimented with making bamboo fly rods, fishing flies, leather quivers, duck decoys, and a variety of other items.

On weekends and sometimes in the evenings, Aldo and Estella took to the woods, fishing, hunting, and camping, their four children in tow. Born in 1927, little Estella soon joined the family troupe in the field, traversing the woods and swamps on her father's shoulders, sleeping in the tent with the rest.

Leopold's tolerance for his job ran short in 1927. He sent out letters to several individuals, inquiring confidentially about positions within the American Game Protective Association, at the University of Wisconsin, and with other organizations. He was seeking the opportunity to establish "an institute for research in game management" and "a training school for administrators of game."[21] The right combination of position, salary, and location did not materialize.

Never one to wait for life to meet him, Leopold pursued other options simultaneously. The Wisconsin land of the late 1920s was only a ghost of what it had been a hundred years earlier. The great pineries of the north had been sliced to nubbins with few replantings to replace them. Many of the marshes and wetlands had been drained or burned for farming. The tallgrass prairies and the oak savannahs had been shaved for crops, roads, and towns. As a forester, Leopold realized that this loss of landscape variety could be somewhat rectified by an effective forestry program. So, with Leopold at the helm, the state's Izaak Walton League swayed public opinion and gained state funds for a forestry and conservation department, with a citizen-run Conservation Commission. Leopold pinned some career hopes on being chosen the department director.

Robert A. McCabe family

*Stumps of white pine litter a farm field near Plainfield, Wisconsin. Leopold took this photograph to document the land's history; it illustrates that soils suited to support hundred-year-old pines were not suited to growing annual row crops.*

A number of well-respected Wisconsinites encouraged the governor to appoint Leopold director. The governor chose someone else—Leopold would not bring him enough political nosegays.

Faced with this further disappointment, Leopold took stock of his professional life. He was forty years old and in a dead-end job. In February of 1928, he applied for and was granted a leave of absence from the lab to think over his options and finish "Southwestern Game Fields." He set himself up as a forest consultant and let the word spread: he was open to full-time job offers.

Options appeared. The position that interested Leopold most—from the Sporting Arms and Ammunitions Manufacturers' Institute (SAAMI)—was the most risky. (He wrote to Estella, "I must have an instinct for poker even though I don't play it."[22]) An organization of gun and ammunition manufacturers, SAAMI recognized that continued sales of sporting guns depended on the restoration of game populations. The Institute asked Leopold to do a state-by-state census and history of game species, and to evaluate the effectiveness of each state's conservation efforts. A big jump in salary was part of the offer. However, if SAAMI disliked Leopold's methods or results, the organization could drop him like a used cartridge.

Leopold accepted. He initiated his first official survey on July 1, 1928. There was a method to his approach. In each state, he searched through public files, inspected the land, and talked to hundreds of people: scientists, farmers, hunters, bird watchers, business owners, museum volunteers, politicians, foresters, and conservation officers. It was a huge job, accomplished quickly and, of necessity, haphazardly. No short survey could gather and integrate all the complex information needed to render a complete picture.

After driving through Michigan, Minnesota, and Iowa, however, Leopold could track some trends. He returned to Madison in September to establish an office and write up his findings. He hauled his walnut Leopold Desk into a borrowed room in the University of Wisconsin's Chemistry Building and hired a part-time student, Vivian Horn, as his secretary. "No awkward beginning stenographer ever had a kinder and more considerate boss," she later commented. "[He] complimented me when I did well and passed over my mistakes lightly, or overlooked them altogether."[23] The stream of work evaporated while he was away and cascaded with his arrival. "I was astounded at the amount of data he could collect and how steadily he could work assembling the data and turning out reports after his return."[24]

Leopold basked in his brief stint at home. He had missed Estella and the children immensely, especially the infant Estella. In August, he had written from Iowa City, "Tonight I keep seeing the baby's portrait. Do you think she'll remember me? Of, course, I don't expect it."[25]

Leopold hit the road again in October, this time with a partner—

Herbert L. Stoddard, a field scientist and member of the U.S. Biological Survey. (In 1924, Stoddard had begun the nation's first scientifically controlled game-management study, on bobwhite quail in Georgia.) For three weeks, Leopold and Stoddard journeyed through seven states, surveying the varying conservation situations. Leopold focused on the interviews, Stoddard on the field inspections. They recognized mutual goals and complimentary skills, and they forged a strong, lifelong friendship.

*Milwaukee Public Museum*

*Herbert L. Stoddard working at the Milwaukee Public Museum in the 1920s. He wrote of Leopold: "I could see at once that we were kindred spirits. We shared almost identical interests. . . . He had a stimulating personality, and in conversation he was able to draw out the thoughts of others, as well as freely sharing the depths of his own brilliant mind."*[26]

Leopold completed the first of his SAAMI reports in time for the 15th Annual American Game Conference in December of 1928. He took the train to Washington, D.C., to deliver his assessments. The conservation societies, sporting groups, and game-management agencies in attendance were awaiting his results; more than a few hunting laws were riding on them.

From its inception, the game-protection movement had been split. Some members felt the only way to protect and promote game was to breed animals on farms, and charge hunters for the meat and the privilege of shooting on farm grounds. Modeled on European techniques, the game farm plan was profitable and required no change in land use. (Two years hence, many members of this contingent would break away from the AGPA to form a group called the More Game Birds for America Foundation.) Others argued for establishing conservation practices to maintain wild game numbers, so hunting could remain natural, free, and democratic—not reserved for those who could pay to join the club. These AGPA members favored refuges, predator control, and some hunting restrictions.

In addition to the politely warring factions within the American Game Protective Association, there were the protectionists outside the organization who were calling for the abolition of hunting. William T. Hornaday still led this battalion.

In the past, these divergent groups had worked together to establish a federal system of refuges and public hunting grounds, but cooperation was eroding. No group had as yet done the research necessary to propel their arguments to the fore.

Leopold's survey findings delivered a challenge to both factions dedicated to saving wild game. His studies showed a clear connection between species populations and the availability of food and cover. Wherever there was "clean farming"—land empty of trees, bushes, ponds, or weed patches against the fence rows—there were fewer game and nongame species. Species survival depended on sufficient habitat nationwide for the animals to feed, hide, and nest. No refuge could sustain a game population if the surrounding farms, forests, and public lands were clean of habitat. Simply limiting or prohibiting hunting would not address this problem; a species without a habitat could not be saved.

Any workable proposals, however, would have to do more than restore habitat. They would have to take into account the complexities of ten-year cycles in populations; of variations in food, cover, and soil preferences; of fluctuations in planting and harvesting times; and of pressure from exotic species: all of these affected game. Leopold explained that the only course to understanding these factors and fashioning effective policies was research. In addition, he proposed that professional game managers be trained in scientific procedures and apprised of up-to-date research; in this way, they could make decisions based on a deeper knowledge of cause and effect, and of the interrelationships between factors.

Discussion erupted before Leopold could step down from the platform. The AGPA members elected him to a new committee responsible for writing up a national game policy. The committee would encompass several of the most respected and dedicated men in game conservation—colleagues with whom Leopold had worked on other ventures—including Carlos Avery, Paul Redington, P. S. Lovejoy, and Fred Pettit. Together, they would draw up a list of priorities for national leadership to tackle in the preservation of America's wildlife.

After the conference, Leopold presented his survey reports to his SAAMI sponsors. They were sufficiently impressed by his conclusions to fund in-depth research projects, allowing him to work with Stoddard to select the most promising researchers in the nation and oversee their projects. They also granted Leopold permission to focus on surveying the north-central states in greater detail.

Upon achieving his objectives in Washington, Leopold returned to Madison for the winter. He prepared for his next survey, gave lectures at the University of Wisconsin in game management, and organized his notes to complete the writing of "Southwestern Game Fields." He sent it to a publisher. The response was a rejection.

After considering the editor's input and the comments of his colleagues, Leopold scaled down the focus to "Deer Management in the Southwest." Unfortunately, the game management methods used in the Southwest—hunting restrictions, predator control, and game refuges—had proved so successful at increasing populations that they had been self-defeating. Over the last few years, reports had been coming to Leopold from the Southwest describing exploding deer populations. The herds in the forest reserves, especially on the Grand Canyon's Kaibab Plateau, had grown so large that they were eating away saplings and ground cover, and dying of malnutrition.

The solution would either be to bring back wolves and mountain lions to trim deer numbers, or build roads to make hunting more accessible and convenient. Years later, Leopold described the situation: "The Gila deer herd, by then wolfless and all but lionless, soon multiplied beyond reason. . . . The deer had so eaten out the range that reduction of the herd was imperative. Here my sin against the wolf caught up with me. The Forest Service . . . ordered the construction of a new road splitting my wilderness area in two."[27] The road and the humans it brought damaged the wilderness as wolves and mountain lions never could.

In 1929, however, Leopold did not have enough data to state publicly that predator control was a mistake. He did see, though, that he couldn't do an accurate job of assessing southwestern deer management from Madison. So he abandoned the project. Instead he began assembling information for a textbook on the emerging field of game management, integrating the wildlife histories, ideas, theories, and methods of game management he himself had researched or applied with information from zoology, biology, and ecology, and examples from scientific field studies such as Stoddard's.

For the next two years, Leopold traveled for his survey research, hammered out game policy positions, wrote articles, and worked on his two manuscripts, *Report on a Game Survey of the North Central States* for SAAMI and *Game Management*. His tendency to push himself too hard once again caught up with him; he endured a ten-day stay in the hospital, which he made productive by dictating portions of the game policy to a young field scientist, Paul Errington, who had received SAAMI research funding.

It was a time of financial insecurity for Leopold and the nation. After the stockmarket crash of 1929, no one took the next paycheck for granted, least of all Leopold. When times were lean, Aldo and his family depended on the Leopold Desk Company stocks he held, as well as on Estella's careful management. (There were times when Aldo's budgetary judgement exasperated her; he once purchased a $300 shotgun when she needed a washing machine.)

By 1930, a game policy for the AGPA had taken shape through Leopold's momentum and guidance. Among many other elements, the policy established these priorities:

- Wildlife habitats on public and private lands had to be preserved and restored through the cooperation of landowners, government agencies, conservation organizations, and sporting groups.
- Money and time had to be set aside to train game-management specialists and carry out research.
- Farmers had to be encouraged to raise game wild on their property as an additional crop. The farmers should then be paid for allowing hunting on their land, and the animals could be hunted as regular game whenever they left the farm property.
- Nongame species of wildlife, barring predators, were important and had to be conserved with the same vigor and through the same policies as game.

Aware of the opposition the policy would meet, Leopold wrote an explanatory article to AGPA members entitled "Game Policy in a Nutshell." In it, he said:

> We conservationists are the doctors of the game supply. We have many ideas as to what needs to be done, and these ideas quite naturally conflict. We are in danger of pounding the table about them, instead of going out on the land and giving them a trial. . . . The Committee which drafted the tentative document . . . included as many diverse opinions as any other group of sportsmen. . . . A vote for the adoption of this policy is, in my opinion, a vote for the idea of experimentation, rather than a vote for any one of the particular systems to be experimented with.[28]

At the 17th Annual American Game Conference, AGPA members voted yes to experimentation and to the majority of the policy decisions. Leopold made national news. *Time* magazine reported that President Hoover, author of *A Remedy for Disappearing Game Fishes*, acknowledged the importance of the new AGPA policy by sending a telegram:

"THE PROTECTION AND PROPAGATION OF THE

USEFUL WILD LIFE OF THE COUNTRY IS OF MUCH GREATER IMPORTANCE THAN IS GENERALLY REALIZED. . . . BIOLOGICAL FACTS SHOULD BE FIRST ASCERTAINED AND MEASURES PLANNED IN ACCORDANCE WITH THEM."[29]

The article included a photograph of Leopold, captioned with the quotation: "Let farmers be game-keepers."[30]

History was made, and a course was set. The AGPA's national strategy would guide wildlife professionals for the next forty years.

In the spring of 1931, Leopold's *Report on a Game Survey of the North Central States* was published; the volume sold for five dollars a copy. Its preface explained the report's purpose:

> . . . to appraise the chances for the practice of game management as a means to game restoration in the north central region. It attempts to describe game conditions as they exist, the opportunities which those conditions offer, the human machinery available for acting on them, and the probable consequences of their neglect.[31]

It was the first work to examine the relationship between game and their habitat in such scope and depth; it provided a jump start to research and professional training in the emerging field of game management. Reviews were favorable. *Hunter-Trader-Trapper* magazine told readers "It would help the wildlife restoration movement mightily if every man who takes a gun afield could study and apply the contents of this fine volume."[32] Hornaday pronounced it "very excellent"; at the same time, he felt it was a hopeless venture—Leopold was "bucking against the impossible."[33] But conservationist P. S. Lovejoy claimed that "game management in America is going to 'date' from it."[34]

Preservationist critics argued that the *Report* and the new national game policy proved Leopold cared little for preserving species, he only wanted more game to shoot. Responding in *The Condor* magazine, Leopold explained that a national game policy could not be built on the assumption that "America consisted of 120 million ornithologists"; the "unpleasant fact [was] that America consists largely of business men, farmers, and Rotarians, busily playing the national game of economic expansion."[35] He pointed out that most people learn about and come to love nature through farming, nature studies, or hunting. If those who are willing to pay to conserve wildlife are hunters, then conservationists must work with them, not against them. If hunting became illegal, Leopold granted, some game species might be saved temporarily. But where would they live? he asked. Who would have paid to save their habitats?

Leopold never lied to himself about his motives or about the dilemmas of conservation:

> I realize, that every time I turn on an electric light . . . I am 'selling out' to the enemies of conservation. When I submit these thoughts to a printing press, I am helping to cut down the woods. When I pour cream in my coffee, I am helping to drain a marsh for cows to graze, and to exterminate the birds of Brazil. . . . What to do? I see only two courses open to the likes of us. One is to go live on locusts in the wilderness, if there is any wilderness left.[36]

The other, he explained, is to help businesses and consumers become conservation-minded so they find ways to enjoy some comforts of modern life without ruining the land.

Leopold firmly believed for years that if people depended on restrictive laws of the government to do their conserving for them, game conservation would fail. Each person had to act with "a respect for living things. No man who would rather see a dead deer than a living one, no man who has not the profound belief in the doctrine of 'Live and let live' has any right himself to live in a world so full of glorious living creatures."[37]

After completing the *Report*, Leopold worked nearly nonstop on *Game Management*, which he saw as a companion volume. He even mustered the children into the effort. (At the time, Starker was eighteen years old, Luna, sixteen, Nina, fourteen, Carl, twelve, and Estella, four.) Aldo set up a Remington typewriter on the dining room table, and those who could took turns pecking away at the index with one finger or two.

Prospects for publishing *Game Management* were hardly promising. Banks had crashed. Companies had folded. People stood in lines all over the country, hoping for a job, or at the very least, a cup of soup. Even so, Leopold kept doggedly at the project between his surveying trips for SAAMI.

Leopold took fewer trips now, because SAAMI had cut back on funds. Before the money could run out altogether, Leopold organized a joint effort between a group of farmers and one of hunters in Dane County, Wisconsin, to raise wild game (with some initial stocking) using land management methods—establishing food plots, shelters, grape tangles, rose clumps, and windbreaks. The farmers supplied the land for the Riley Game Cooperative, and the hunters provided the feed and some of the labor. They also paid the farmers a use fee to hunt, as the AGPA game policy recommended.

Robert A. McCabe family

*The 1,700-acre Riley Game Cooperative, also called the Riley Shooting Preserve. Leopold took this photograph in September 1944, after some of the shelter plantings and other habitat features had had time to grow. In an essay describing the success of the venture, Leopold wrote: "It was a pleasant thing that first spring, as we strolled over these formerly gameless farms, to hear quail whistling in every fence-row and pheasant cocks crowing all over the Sugar Creek Marsh."*[38]

The experiment succeeded beyond expectations. Wild populations of grouse, prairie chicken, and pheasant increased naturally on these farms, and the hunters bagged their agreed-upon limits each fall.

Spurred on by the questions his survey had raised about wildlife population cycles, Leopold attended an international conference on the subject in Matamek, Quebec, in July 1931. It was a high-powered convention, and Leopold made the acquaintance of a wide range of scientists whose work would influence him from this point on. Most notable was Charles Elton, a young British pioneer in zoology and the author of *Animal Ecology*, a book examining the complex relationships between animal species.

Leopold had been using the term "ecology" since 1920, but the subject was still relatively new to him, as it was to most American scientists. The term evolved from two Greek words: "oikos," often translated as "household" or "home," and "logos," which means knowledge. In 1860, the German scientist Ernst Haeckel defined ecology as the "domestic side of organic life"[39]—a study of patterns in how species relate to their home or to each other.

Researchers had been studying plant ecology at the Universities of Chicago and Nebraska since 1921, and some American universities were taking an interest in animal ecology. Leopold used the word "ecological" in a more far expansive way, to refer to the relationships between all inhabitants and their habitat: animal, plant, and soil ecologies studied together. The field of land ecology had no precedent—yet.

The conference magnified Leopold's vision of the land's complexity: instead of a body with many parts, it was a community with many groups and individuals affecting each other.

As rapidly as Leopold was strengthening his scientific understanding, he was establishing international contacts and gaining public recognition. In the fall of 1931, *Outdoor Life* magazine awarded him its gold medal for conservation. Yet he still lacked a publisher for *Game Management*. Finally, Charles Scribner's Sons agreed to publish the manuscript if Leopold would contribute five hundred dollars to defray production costs.

On his forty-fifth birthday, Aldo signed the contract. He solicited comments on the manuscript from experts in various fields, and revised the text again, updating and refining it. The process took six months. Before sending the final draft to Scribners, he dedicated the book to his father, a "pioneer in sportsmanship," and added the poetic quotation:

How oft against the sunset sky or moon
We watched the moving zig-zag of spread wings,
In unforgotten autumns gone too soon,
In unforgettable springs.[40]

The preface that followed explained how game management fit into the context of society's goals:

> We of the industrial age boast of our control over nature. Plant or animals, star or atom, wind or river—there is no force on earth or sky which we do not shortly harness to build 'the good life' for ourselves. But what is the good life? . . . Man cannot live by bread, or Fords, alone. Are we too poor in purse or spirit to apply some of it to keep the land pleasant to see, and good to live in? . . . The central thesis of game management is this: game can be restored by the creative use of the same tools which have heretofore destroyed it—axe, plow, cow, fire, and gun.[41]

The guts of *Game Management* used graphs, charts, studies, and scientific explanations to demonstrate how game could be restored using such tools. Then, in the book's last paragraph, Leopold revealed his dream for the profession of game management—the transformation of society:

> In short, twenty centuries of 'progress' have brought the average citizen a vote, a national anthem, a Ford, a bank account, and a high opinion of himself, but not the capacity to live in high density without befouling and denuding his environment, nor a conviction that such capacity, rather than such density, is the true test of whether he is civilized. The practice of game management may be one of the means of developing a culture which will meet this test.[42]

In the midst of the rewriting, SAAMI funds ran out. Leopold, the renowned game scientist, was out of a job. He had stationery printed, and once again, set about advertising his services as a consulting forester. Estella tightened the household budget. After sending off his manuscript in July, Leopold found temporary jobs helping different state agencies and private organizations manage their land to attract wildlife. No permanent job turned up.

*University of Wisconsin–Madison Archives X25 2950*

*Estella with teenaged Starker and little Stella. While Aldo was putting out his shingle as a consulting forester, Estella kept the house running smoothly. She did her work with poise, acumen, graciousness, and good humor (she no doubt developed some of these talents as a young schoolteacher). All of these qualities were required when the wilder of her children were running the neighbor's lawn chairs up flag poles, taking dangerous risks ice sailing, flunking out of classes, and so forth.*

Throughout the rest of 1932 and 1933, Leopold talked to various university officials about establishing a teaching position in game management. But to most people, the crisis in the banks seemed more pressing than the wildlife crisis. No funds came through. The family lived off Leopold Desk Company stocks and money Aldo's father had left him.

In May 1933, Aldo held a bound volume of *Game Management.* He sent a signed copy to W. T. Hornaday with a note: "My whole venture into this field dates from your visit to Albuquerque in 1915, and your subsequent encouragement to stay in it."[43]

*Game Management,* like its companion *Report on a Game Survey,* found favor with scientists, sportsmen, and conservationists. It introduced terms such as "nesting densities," "radius of mobility," "environment," and "edge effect" into the national vocabulary. Money from royalties came trickling in soon after. Leopold used the first of it for a "much needed blow-out for the family."[44]

The burden of the Great Depression had not yet lightened. Long-term drought and gigantic wind storms had begun turning the Southwest Farm Belt into a dust-rasped desert. The grazing and farming practices Leopold had sought to change had left the topsoil unprotected, the land vulnerable.

Library of Congress

*Poor land and economic practices, aggravated by drought, brought on the miseries of the Dust Bowl. Leopold wrote: "There is no doubt that a society rooted in the soil is more stable than one rooted in pavements."*[45]

Franklin Delano Roosevelt, the new president, saw the depth of the destruction and its repercussions. His statement, "The Nation that destroys its soil destroys itself," became the basis for his conservation work program, the Civilian Conservation Corps (CCC). One of its major goals was to keep the nation's topsoil in place. The government asked Leopold to assist in running the CCC in the Southwest for the summer. He didn't hesitate.

Back in his beloved Southwest, Leopold found his theories about erosion confirmed. He had seen these lands before overgrazing made them vulnerable to destruction, and he had tried to change the tide of events then. But to no avail. Public opinion still looked at the Dust Bowl as a merciless act of God rather than as a result of human shortsightedness.

Leopold spent the summer trying to direct the CCC's erosion control efforts and updating his *Watershed Handbook.* The alphabet soup of agencies at work on the land, and the confusion of their efforts, disheartened him. He later described a similar project run by too many conservation groups: "The new creek bed is ditched straight as a ruler; it has been uncurled by the county engineer to hurry the run-off. On the hill in the background are contoured strip-crops; they have been 'curled' by the erosion engineer to retard the run-off. The water must be confused by so much advice."[46]

Mix-ups like those he had been witnessing in his CCC work, he wrote, were common and self-destructive:

> Such crossed wires were frequent, even in CCC camps where crews were directed by brainy young technicians, many of them fresh from conservation schools, but each schooled only in his particular specialty. . . . The plain lesson is that to be a practitioner of conservation on a piece of land takes more brains, and a wider range of sympathy, forethought, and experience, than to be a specialized forester, game manager, range manager, or erosion expert in a college or conservation bureau. Integration is easy on paper, but a lot more important and more difficult in the field than any of us foresaw.[47]

During this time, Leopold made one of the most significant speeches of his career. The Southwestern Division of the American Association for the Advancement of Science invited him to present the fourth annual John Wesley Powell Lecture in Las Cruces, New Mexico. In his speech, "The Conservation Ethic," Leopold gave voice to some of the ideas that had been simmering in him for years. The land is made up of a community of animals, plants, and soils, he said, and civilization is built upon this community. Decisions about land guided only by self-interest, technology, and economics have resulted in destruction. He argued that if we want our civilization to survive, our relationship with nature must be governed by stable, long-sighted principles. Ethics, moral codes, and culture will have to evolve to the point of embracing the land community. "Civilization is not . . . the enslavement of a stable and constant earth," he said. "It is a state of *mutual and interdependent cooperation* between human animals, other animals, plants, and soils, which may be disrupted at any time by the failure of any of them."[48]

If all citizens understood their place in the scheme, Leopold theorized, they would become responsible in their businesses, in their purchases, on their farms, and in the voting booth. Anyone who lived on a piece of land would begin to perceive his or her part in the "raising" of wild plants and animals. "A rare bird or flower need remain no rarer than the people willing to venture their skill in building it a habitat."[49]

Leopold explained that such land ethics could begin in the personal husbandry of each landowner, especially each farmer: "Bread and beauty grow best together. Their harmonious integration can make farming not only a business but an art; the land not only a food factory but an instrument of self-expression, on which each can play music of his own choosing."[50]

In this address, Leopold made the jump publicly from speaking of society's norms and laws to the values of a culture and the choices of its individuals; from policies for public lands to the moral use of private lands; from the economics of self-interest to land-based, community-centered ethics; from tampering with the status quo to taking a divergent path toward a more harmonious future. In this speech, he wove together the aesthetic appreciation and morals of his childhood into the knowledge he had acquired through his various careers as forester, city planner, public relations professional, game-protection activist, inspector, erosion technician, scientist, and researcher. Leopold was moving away from a position of confident manager of the land to one of a humble, observing steward.

Leopold had no time to pursue this line of thinking further. As he often said, "Breakfast comes before ethics."[51] The task still at hand was to find a stable job.

# The Land Laboratories
# 1933-1936

*Every farm is a textbook on animal ecology;*
*woodsmanship is the translation of the book.*

*"Home Range,"* A Sand County Almanac

On June 26, 1933, the University of Wisconsin offered Aldo Leopold a position teaching the nation's first graduate program in game management. The *New York Times* hailed it as the "one and only 'wild-game chair.'"[1]

This was the chance he'd been waiting for. Despite the small salary, Leopold accepted. Letters of congratulation filled the mailbox at 2222 Van Hise. Among them was one from none other than the preservationist crusader, W. T. Hornaday:

> My Dear Ally,
> I salute the University of Wisconsin, for its foresight and enterprise in establishing the first Collegiate Professorship of Game Management created in the United States. . . . I congratulate the Wisconsin Alumni Foundation on its correct initiative in the choice of the Best Man for the new foundation. . . . It is all a helpful gesture in the struggle to save American game and sport from finally going over the precipice, A.D. 1940.[2]

Leopold set up shop in "two small, rather dark rooms"[3] in the basement of the university's Soils Building. As an outsider to the academic establishment, he was expected to be more of a free-floating conservation resource for the state than a departmental teacher. He outlined some of his duties for the *Milwaukee Journal:*

> To conduct research in the life history of Wisconsin birds and mammals; develop cropping methods suitable for their preservation and increase; train men to devise and apply such methods; impart to other students a general understanding of the wild life conservation problem; assist farmers and other landowners in selecting and applying cropping methods; integrate game with other uses of land; and advise conservation officers on questions of wild life management and policy.[4]

He was charged with giving radio talks and public addresses, overseeing soil-erosion and game-cropping projects, and helping plan a university arboretum and wildlife refuge—all before the official teaching would begin.

Since conservation was "a way of living on land"[5] for Leopold, he wanted to involve as many people as possible. He recruited high-school conservation groups to work with him on wildlife research, and he gave farmers radio pep talks on how to convert their land into something more than just a business venture—something beautiful and sustainable:

> There are many little tricks for increasing the service of woods and vegetation to wildlife. . . . Our own place in the scheme of things is not the less tolerable for making room for a few of our fellow creatures. . . . Your woodlot is in fact, a historical document which faithfully records your personal philosophy. Let it tell a story of tolerance toward living things, and of skill in the greatest of arts: how to use the earth without making it ugly.[6]

These radio talks carried such titles as: "Plant Evergreens for Bird Shelters," "Wildflower Corners," "The Farm Woodlot Crop," and "The Bird Crop."

Eighty-year-old Stoughton Faville, a farmer and naturalist in Jefferson County, Wisconsin, liked Leopold's approach. With the help of his farm manager, Faville organized a group of farmers willing to turn their acres into a land laboratory. Some of them, such as Sam Kisow, had been experimenting with wild pheasant cropping for a few years. Under Leopold's guidance, these dedicated landowners eventually established the Faville Grove Wildlife Experimental Area, where farmers and students worked together on wild game cropping with quail, pheasants, and Hungarian partridges. They researched the food value of prairie species and studied the effects that food plots, windbreaks, grape tangles, and plantings of yellow willows and rose clumps had on wildlife populations.

In the face of increasing erosion across the state and the nation,

Robert A. McCabe family (photo by Aldo Leopold)

*A crew combing a hay field to count nests at Faville Grove. Most game birds in southern Wisconsin favored hay fields for nesting, so this was an effective way of monitoring changes in populations.*

Leopold labored to set up a working model of community soil conservation and land use that was harmonious with wildlife. (The days when he had supported development projects which worked against the land, such as draining the Rio Grande Valley, were long gone.) In Coon Valley, Wisconsin, he persuaded 315 farmers to put in their lot for 5 years with the combined forces of the CCC, the SES, and Leopold and other university specialists to make the model a successful reality. (Both Luna and Starker worked on the Coon Valley project, Luna in conjunction with his studies at the University of Wisconsin,[7] and Starker during a hiatus from them.) Leopold hoped this coordinated approach would short-circuit the confusion that occurred in the Southwest among the various conservation entities and their disparate goals.

It worked. The farmers voluntarily experimented with contour plowing, strip cropping, and rotations. They fenced off steep slopes from livestock, planted conifers (as well as native shrubs and grasses), replanted banks and slopes, and repaired gullies. In addition, they employed some wild-game-cropping techniques. The five-year Coon Valley project, which Leopold dubbed "an adventure in cooperative conservation,"[8] served as a demonstration for the nation. A year after the project began, the quail population had doubled, the topsoil was a step more stable, and the landscape was growing more varied and beautiful.

On January 2, 1934, Leopold stood in front of his first set of students—not graduate students, but eighteen young farmers ready to learn the business of wild game cropping. He did not carry the air of an academic expert, and there was not a "Dr." before his name. Instead, the young farmers faced an ordinary-looking man with laugh lines, rimless spectacles, a blue-gray gaze, a field tan, and a deep, gentle voice that was easy to listen to. One student later wrote, "He impressed me as a man; he carried himself with the grace of an athlete, slightly built but finely coordinated, quick of eye, ever ready with a smile, impeccably attired, neatly groomed."[9]

None of his students would have guessed that Leopold had just been appointed to a presidential committee. The record-breaking droughts of the early 1930s had caused such a decline in duck populations that hunters and conservationists alike pressured President Roosevelt to do something. On the opening day of Leopold's class, the president announced that he had

*Ding Darling. When Darling took over the Biological Survey, most waterfowl populations were at one of their lowest points ever. His leadership in restoring wetlands averted near extinction for many species. He created the art for some of the first annual Duck Stamps.*

formed a Committee on Wild Life Restoration and that three prominent conservationists would serve on it: Thomas Beck, chairman of the Connecticut State Board of Fisheries and Game, and editor of *Collier's Weekly* magazine; Jay "Ding" Darling, a Pulitzer-Prize-winning cartoonist and conservationist; and Aldo Leopold. The group of three men, assigned to create a plan for conserving the nation's wildlife, became known as the Beck Committee, earning the nickname the "Duck Committee."

The committee met with President Roosevelt at the end of January. Luna recalled that his Dad thought "Roosevelt was one of the most impressive men he had ever talked to."[10] Though Leopold didn't feel that taxpayers should pay for reversing the damage individual landowners had wracked on their land, he did agree with the president that a federal refuge system was essential.

After the meeting, the three men worked to identify marginal, low-cost farmlands to buy up for refuges. Beck, who belonged to the More Game Birds crowd, wanted to acquire areas that could be easily adapted to raising waterfowl in incubators. In contrast, Leopold and Darling argued for encouraging landowners to make their lands more habitable for wild game and for purchasing acres that could be easily restored to their natural habitats.

The committee stalled. Darling finally took all the notes home and wrote a compromise proposal. The nine-point plan called for the initial purchase of twelve million acres, with more money and land to be allotted later.

The National Wildlife Refuge System, as a system, was off to a shaky start, but a start nonetheless. Soon after the report was issued, Ding Darling was chosen to oversee the U.S. Biological Survey. This scientific agency orchestrated species censuses, predator control, and migratory waterfowl regulations. As its director, Darling would oversee the refuge system.

Robert A. McCabe family

*"Pheasant on slippery ice"—a slide taken and used by Professor Leopold in the classroom. From the amount of spacing between the tracks on the lower left, he explained, one could tell that the pheasant had been running across the snow-covered ice. Then the pheasant slipped and fell on its tail. When it got up, it thought better of its fast pace and walked the rest of the distance.*

Darling's strong leadership and his innovative development of the Duck Stamp for revenue helped the National Wildlife Refuge System send down lasting roots into the wetlands of America.

In March 1934, Leopold first offered Course 118 in Game Management to the university students. There were no required textbooks—the nearby woods, swamps, and fields took their place. No one ventured to class without binoculars, warm clothes, and boots. On days too cold to keep the binoculars steady, Professor Leopold projected field photographs onto the classroom wall with a slide lantern, passing around mimeographed copies of his hand-drawn maps, diagrams, and charts.

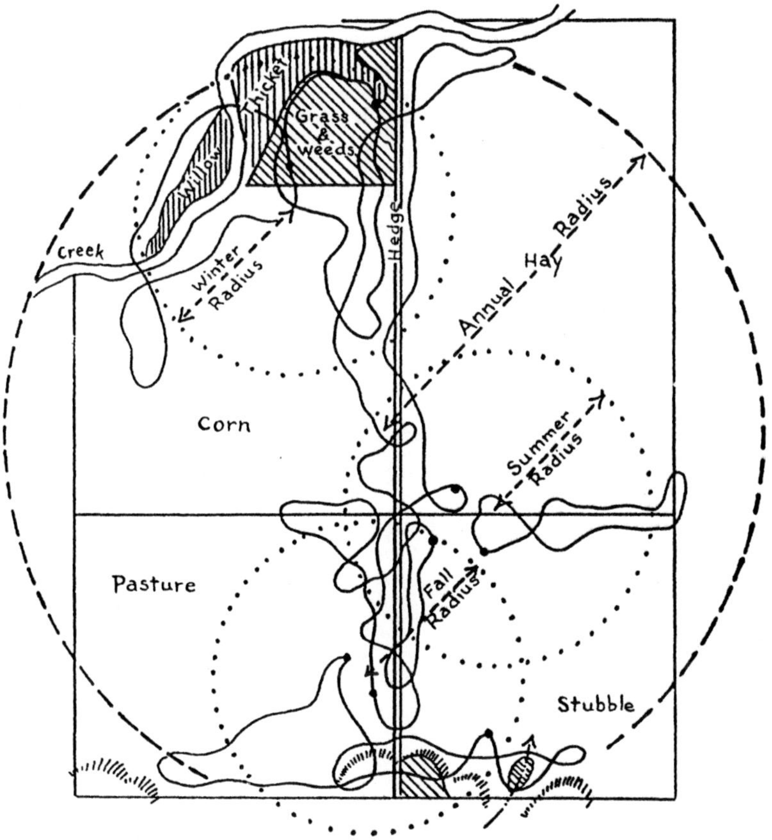


Robert A. McCabe family

*One of Leopold's mimeographed class handouts. It shows the home range of a covey of quail and how it changes with seasons based on food and cover availability.*

That spring, Leopold accepted his first graduate student. The course catalog for the agricultural college warned: "There is no formal instruction. . . . The student takes the initiative in selecting and executing the work, with consultation from the instructor."[11] Franklin Schmidt came to Leopold after three years' research at the Chicago Field Museum and five at the University of Wisconsin. Prairie chickens were his passion. Quiet, intense, and dedicated, Frank would venture into a rare stand of prairie grasses and remain on watch for a month at a time. He needed neither shack nor shower—a bedroll and a drainage ditch kept him "clean and respectable."[12] He carried his laboratory on his back: notepads, pencils, dissecting instruments, and binoculars.

Schmidt required very little guidance. Like a migrating bird, he used the university, and Leopold, as a resting and nurturing stop between his travels. Leopold said of his student, "He knew more about the life and history and ecology of the prairie grouse [chicken] than any living man, and as much as any living ecologist could know about any American game bird."[13]

While Schmidt was studying in the prairies, Leopold and the other faculty members on the interdisciplinary Arboretum Committee were working on plans to rebuild one. The group had decided against a traditional park with imported ornamental trees in favor of a plan to reconstruct a sample of Wisconsin's lands before settlement.

A 245-acre run-down farm near the south shore of Lake Wingra was selected by the faculty committee as the base of the experiment. (They would add more acres as the farm crisis of the 1930s made the surrounding lands available at prices the university could afford. By 1942, the arboretum would encompass 1,100 acres.) The majority of the land had been cleared, plowed, and drained, as had most of Wisconsin. At the very least, the planners realized, it would take decades to rebuild the original land communities—prairies, marshes, hardwood forests, and pine woods. And first, workers would have to rescue from the onslaught of plow and pavement as many native plant and animal species as possible from other parts of the state. This work would require dedication, field detective work, and serendipitous sweeps of good fortune—to find those rare species hidden along railroad tracks, in old cemeteries, and between abandoned

*The arboretum lands before restoration efforts. Other leaders in the planning of the arboretum included botanists Norman Fassett and John Curtis and landscape designer G. William Longenecker. Curtis Prairie, one of the arboretum's first prairies, is the world's oldest restored tallgrass prairie.*

junkers on farmers' lots.

On June 17, 1934, state and local leaders sat quietly in an old barn waiting for the dedication of the university's newest and grandest experiment. "The time has come for science to busy itself with the earth itself," Leopold explained to the crowd in his dedication speech. "The first step is to reconstruct a sample of what we had to start with. That, in a nutshell, is the Arboretum."[14] Beyond this, Leopold and his colleagues hoped to provide visitors a living exhibit of "what ought to be."[15]

After Leopold's speech, Chief Albert Yellow Thunder, in traditional Winnebago dress, stood up. "My people are like the trees," he said, "a dying race, leaving behind them as their only monument the natural forests and streams of America."[16] Like the wolf, the Winnebago might never return in great numbers, but the land would tell their story.

Yellow Thunder's words cut deep. "Progress" had banished not only the original land communities, but also those peoples who had lived as part of them.

Labor on the arboretum followed. Crews of CCC workers assisted in preparing the land and transplanting the native species. The importance of this land experiment grew daily. One of the worst ecological disasters in the history of the world was still playing itself out in the Midwest—the drought was merciless. The hot winds of summer dragged millions of bushels of topsoil off farms and flung the dirt in the faces of a tired, worn-out nation. Most homes were destitute; few had full pantries. The Leopolds offered what they could when they met others with less. They played Secret Santa for one farm family each Christmas until the family's fortune improved.

In the fall of 1934, a small group of conservationists, angered by the land destruction and excessive development they witnessed daily, and inspired by Leopold's writings, decided "to organize an aggressive society for the preservation of wilderness."[17] The four men—Bob Marshall, Benton MacKaye, Harvey Broome, and Bernard Frank—invited carefully selected individuals to join them. Aldo Leopold topped the list. Marshall called him "the Commanding General of the Wilderness Battle."[18]

Despite commitments to other conservation and science organizations, Leopold was "more than glad to serve."[19] Thus the Wilderness Society was born. The eight founding members, with Bob Marshall in the lead,

The Wilderness Society

*Benton MacKaye, Bob Marshall, Mable Abercrombie, and Harvey Broome—some of the founding members of the Wilderness Society—enjoy the Smokies at Mt. Kephart in January 1936. Though Abercrombie was not a founder, she was an early member.*

created a conservation workhorse.

While Marshall organized his society of "spirited individuals," two counties in Wisconsin staged the nation's first bow-hunting deer season in a hundred years. Aldo, Estella, Starker, and Luna tracked twelve bucks through light, new-winter snow. Their arrows flew wide, far, narrow, and short. But they had such a rousing good time they decided to look for some old farmland to buy for a future base camp.

The land hunt went on through the winter. In January 1935, shortly after his birthday, Aldo cornered his quarry. It was an abandoned farm on the Wisconsin River, near Baraboo. In the middle of a blizzard, he piled everyone into the family's two-door Chevy to look upon his treasure.

At first, no one in the family could see what had drawn him to the place other than the low price. A chicken coop with a pile of manure at one end, a forlorn line of elms, bushels of sand blowing and dusting the snow, and a seemingly endless stretch of ruts. Certainly nothing to brag about. Yet the place did have a certain ungainly attraction. The family took to it. They cleaned out the chicken coop, built a fireplace, and raised the roof. In April, after renting for three months, the Leopolds made the deal. "The Shack" was theirs.

The spring of 1935 brought the worst dust storms the nation had ever seen—dirt picked up in Kansas fields was hurled over the plains clear

*The Shack in 1935 or 1936. Only a lone line of elderly elms, the stubble of years-old corn, and a few apple trees remained of an earlier farmer's dreams of posterity.*

to the Atlantic. Whirling, pounding, sweeping winds of dirt whistled in people's ears and eyes. Animals died by the hundreds, tiny pebbles clogging their breath and driving into their skins. The dust of the nation sifted down on a Depression-laden land.

Early in July, the Leopolds watched the dust blow around the Shack. Pulling out a fresh brown notebook, Aldo labeled it: *Journal for 1935*. He made a few staccato recordings about the past few months with approximate dates: "Feb 3. Started work on fireplace with Starker and Luna." "May 19. Planted food-patch." "June 20? Yellow lady's-slipper in bloom in Lewis woods."[20] From July first on, though, the journal became more accurate and ongoing. Over the fourth of July weekend, the family was "run out by mosquitoes—went to Baraboo tourist camp for night."[21] (They added a screen door soon after.)

In mid-July, the summer entries end. Estella and young Stella set off to visit Santa Fe, while Aldo and five foresters left for Europe. Their mission: to observe how the Germans and Czecho Slovakians managed their land and wildlife. The expenses were paid by the Oberlaender Trust of the Carl Schurz Memorial Foundation, an organization dedicated to cross-cultural sharing between the United States and German-speaking countries.

With few forest inspections, it was clear to Leopold that the Germans ruled their forests and wildlife with efficiency as their goal. The forests lacked predators, independent wildlife, and the leaf litter that normally decayed into healthy topsoil. Fences surrounded seedlings. Brick banks enclosed rivers. Desired game animals, such as deer, were fed on straw bales.

"We, Americans, have not yet experienced a bearless, wolfless, eagleless, catless woods," Leopold noted after his forest tours. "We yearn for more deer and more pines, and we shall probably get them. But do we realize that to get them, as the Germans have, at the expense of their wild environment and their wild enemies, is to get very little indeed?"[22]

In German forests, spruce was the tree of choice because it grew quickly. Forest after forest had been tamed by the saw into a spruce-tree farm. Over the decades, the buildup of too many spruce needles had tainted the soil with acid, so the foresters had begun to plant a mix of beech, oak, and other hardwoods among the spruce. Their controlled plantings, however, could not bring back the health of the original forest. Leopold wrote:

> I know a hardwood forest called the Spessart, covering a mountain on the north flank of the Alps. Half of it has sustained cuttings since 1605, but was never slashed. The other half was slashed during the 1600s. . . . the [replanted] old slashing now produces only mediocre pine, while the unslashed portion grows the finest cabinet oak in the world. One of those oaks fetches a higher price than a whole acre of old slashings.[23]

The Spessart forest proved dramatically that the European timbering methods Leopold had depended upon as a young forester were too violent. Slash cutting (or clearcutting) entire sections of a forest destroyed the underground communities of "bacteria, molds, fungi, insects, and burrowing animals."[24] In contrast, Leopold observed, if selected trees were cut annually, these forest communities, and the fertility they provided the forest as a whole, could be saved.

"There is an almost uncanny mixture of the admirable with the false in everything one sees here,"[25] Leopold wrote. Though he did not like the results of German forest efficiency, he admitted that the German nation as a whole loved its land.

> Their interest in nature is real. They know about the vegetation, the birds, and the animals they see. Not many of the week-end pilgrims drive automobiles. Even if motoring were less expensive, they would probably prefer to hike rather than drive. These people want to get their feet on the soil. That surging interest in nature impressed me more than anything else in Europe.[26]

The German methods of hunting licensure and farm husbandry especially exemplified this interest. The Germans put a prescriptive emphasis on safe, informed hunting. Hunters were required to take a day-long test covering a district's animals, birds, vegetation, and game laws to receive a license. They also had to pass a safety and marksmanship test. Farmers, without being required to, tended their land with the same breadth and depth of knowledge and committment:

> For the farmers, their land is more than merely a source of livelihood. It is a part of them. Many of them are descendants of families which have lived for generations on the same farm. They and their fathers built up its soil; they know every foot of it and take a personal interest in everything it produces. They know the habits of the birds and animals that live on it—know about the wildflowers and trees and weeds.[27]

A measure of sadness and regret crept into Leopold's observations: sadness that some of the admirable qualities of European land management had not been passed on into contemporary American life, and regret that he had lobbied much of his life for intensive, utilitarian management of forests and wildlife. The German system showed him how destructive this kind of management could be—the land was too complex to be "managed."

Leopold concluded that understanding, rather than control, must be the goal of wildlife specialists. The more humans know about the land community, the less damage they may do to it. "Our tools are better than we are, and they grow faster than we do," he stated in an address on "Engineering and Conservation." "They suffice to crack the atom, to command the tides. But they do not suffice for the oldest task in human history: to live on a piece of land without spoiling it."[28]

The efficiency and control Leopold noticed in the German forests were evident in the society as well. At first, the thousands of smart-looking young men in uniforms of "57 varieties"[29] evoked a clean image of determination. Later, the darker side of German discipline cast its shadow. One of Leopold's hosts was a Jewish professor—Alfred Schottlaender. His relatives had just been sent to a newly formed "camp" in the country. Aldo wrote to Estella, "There is a tragic story behind this family of which I will tell you when I get home."[30]

In November, still in Germany, Leopold received word that Franklin

Schmidt had been killed in a house fire. Frank had run into the blaze to save his mother, and the roof had collapsed. Aldo was "pretty much knocked out" about the news. Franklin had been "a rare and inspiring biologist"[31] as well as a friend.

Once back in America, Leopold encountered a new and invigorating national attitude toward game conservation. Over the summer, under Ding Darling's tutelage, the American Game Protective Association had disbanded and rearranged itself with other groups to become the American Wildlife Institute. The 22nd American Game Conference was canceled, and President Roosevelt called for the first North American Wildlife Conference to be held in February of 1936. Game conservation had finally expanded, by title at least, into wildlife conservation.

At the 1936 conference, Leopold joined Herbert Stoddard and other prominent wildlife biologists and managers to form a professional organization of "Wildlife Specialists." The group eventually became known as "The Wildlife Society." Its aim was to raise the standards of the management profession by promoting a dependency on biological research and knowledge.

Since Aldo's departure for Europe, the Shack had been virtually abandoned. But with his return and the promise of spring, the family set about on the weekends making some improvements. They built benches, bunks, shelves, and a table from pieces of wood that had drifted down the river. "Windows and a door for the Shack, my father found in the local dump," Nina explained. "I find myself smiling as I contemplate Dad, the sophisticated university professor, scrounging through the dump, looking for usable objects."[32] A sturdy outhouse was erected and nicknamed "the Parthenon." The family cooked at the fireplace or in a Dutch oven outdoors; a hand pump outside supplied the water. Oat straw from a neighbor's field filled their mattresses. From the beginning, Aldo had established the firm rule that nothing should ever be brought to the Shack that wasn't *absolutely necessary.*

In April, influenced by the idealistic aims of the arboretum, Aldo decided to try a similar experiment on his own acres. The whole family, from nine-year-old Estella to forty-four-year-old Estella, was drafted into the ranks of tree planters. Aldo ordered a thousand white and a thousand red pines.

The Aldo Leopold Foundation

*Nina toting only the essentials to the Shack: food, school books (rarely opened), a guitar (often used), and a gun.*

The Aldo Leopold Foundation

*Aldo and Estella at work planting at the Shack. "On this sand farm in Wisconsin, first worn out and then abandoned by our bigger-and-better society, we try to rebuild, with shovel and axe, what we are losing elsewhere. It is here that we seek—and still find—our meat from God."*[33]

The sweating started. A neighbor plowed tracks through the sand so the seedlings could be dropped in. The Leopolds bent and tucked. They sowed not only pine, but mountain ash, tamarack, and plum trees along with cranberry, raspberry, juneberry, and nannyberry bushes. The fierce, tight fist of the drought still held back the rains. On the weekends, the Leopolds formed a rescue bucket brigade from the pump to the seedlings, but the sand couldn't hold the moisture. More than three-fourths of the plants died.

The hard work at the Shack took on a less laborious flavor as the summer wore on. The Shack journal hoarded notes of days spent patrolling the grounds, fishing, watching for the first wildflower blooms, or counting nests among the grasses. The whole family hunted, fished, and observed. Everyone had a personal project to work on besides those shared with the

Robert A. McCabe family (photo by Aldo Leopold)

*Starker examines the grape tangle wildlife shelter he and his father constructed at the Shack in April 1936. They felled a dying tree next to a clump of living grape vines and wrapped the vines around the downed limbs, creating an ideal shelter—with food readily available—for small animals.*

University of Wisconsin–Madison Archives X25 115

*A page from Carl's journal showing some of the work that went into making the Shack, the family's "week-end refuge from too much modernity."*[34]

others. Aldo kept in-depth notes of animal sightings, plant placements, and growth measurements. Estella transplanted wildflowers. Starker and Luna mapped their wildlife feeding plots and made careful charts. Carl taught his falcon to hunt for him and collected plants with Nina for their herbarium. Little Estella made mud dams, floated boats down the river, or played with her pet crow. Their dog, Flick, chased rabbits, and the archers had roving target practices. At night, the kids pulled out their guitars and crooned the Spanish canciones they had learned in their childhood.[35]

That fall, in 1936, Aldo and a friend journeyed to the back river canyons of the Sierra Madre range in Chihuahua, Mexico, for a hunting expedition. Though much like the American Southwest, the lush, rough lands of the Rio Gavilan were free of the ditches, gullies, and silted streams that plagued U.S. forests. Mountain lions and wolves still ruled the range. The mesas and riverbanks held wild turkeys, quail, river otters, wild potatoes, golden grasses, gnarled old oaks, and sycamores. Leopold wrote:

> The song of the waters is audible to every ear, but there is other music in these hills, by no means audible to all. To hear even a few notes of it, you must first live here for a long time, and you must know the speech of the hills and rivers. Then on a still night, when the campfire is low . . . Sit quietly and listen for a wolf to howl, and think hard of everything you have seen and tried to understand. Then you may hear it—a vast pulsing harmony—its score inscribed on a thousand hills, its notes the lives and deaths of plants and animals, its rhythms spanning the seconds and centuries.[36]

During the trip, the pieces of the puzzle Leopold had been working on all his life fell into place. He realized that most of his life he had seen only sick land. Only in Mexico had he come upon land communities, or biotas, that were still in perfect health. "The term 'unspoiled wilderness,'" he wrote, "took on new meaning."[37]

From this point on, Leopold's professional focus shifted. His trained eye now sought signs of land health rather than of land sickness, and he guided his ever-growing band of graduate students in this vision. He resolved that the remaining areas of American wilderness had to be saved for science, since technology could never replace what civilization destroyed. "Every region," he proposed, "should retain representative samples of its original wilderness condition, to serve science as a sample of normality. Just as doctors must study healthy people to understand disease, so must the land sciences study the wilderness to understand disorders of the land mechanism."[38]

What makes a land healthy and stable? And what is our part in keeping it that way? The answers howled in a distant woods. In Leopold's mind, the case for preserving predators had finally been won. Land systems were too intricate to be reduced to hunters and a few cropping factors, such as food and cover. He urged wildlife managers to protect *all* the neglected species of a biota, *including* rare plants and predators. He stated:

> The last word in ignorance is the man who says of an animal or plant: 'what good is it?' If the land mechanism as a whole is good, then every part is good, whether we understand it or not. If the biota, in the course of eons, has built something we like but do not understand, then who but a fool would discard seemingly useless parts? To keep every cog and wheel is the first precaution of intelligent tinkering.[39]

To speed the change in management thinking and attitudes, Leopold urged the Wilderness Society and the Wildlife Society to hold joint meetings with the Ecological Society of America, of which he was also a member. All three societies shared basic concerns and policy objectives, and Leopold wanted to encourage them to base their decisions more firmly on ecology and land health—to consider all the cogs and wheels.

Leopold's fight to save remaining stands of wilderness took on new vigor and urgency. In the inaugural issue of *The Living Wilderness* (the journal of the Wilderness Society), Leopold wrote the lead article, "Why a Wilderness Society?" "The long and short of the matter," he synthesized, "is that . . . we do not yet understand and cannot yet control the long-time interrelations of animals, plants, and mother earth. . . . The Wilderness

Society is, philosophically, a disclaimer of the biotic arrogance of *Homo americanus*. It is one of the focal points of a new attitude—an intelligent humility toward man's place in nature."[40]

# The Professor 1937-1939

*The objective is to teach the student to see the land,*
*to understand what he sees, and enjoy what he understands.*
*I say land rather than wildlife,*
*because wildlife cannot be understood*
*without understanding the landscape as a whole.*

*"The Role of Wildlife in a Liberal Education,"*
The River of the Mother of God and Other Essays

The windswept wastelands of the Dust Bowl made it clear to many Americans how fragile the human place in nature is. Suddenly, schools across the country wanted to teach conservation, erosion prevention, and wildlife management. Letters piled up on Leopold's desk, asking his advice. Leopold replied with a list of resources, but his overriding message was that nature was the best teacher.

At fifty-one, Leopold had seven graduate students and a full flock of undergraduates. With a blend of affection and awe, they called him "the Professor."[1] Game Management 118 had become a campus favorite. On Saturdays, the class traveled to the arboretum (which was slowly growing toward a natural state) or to various research plots. In the field, Leopold pointed out such elements as animal tracks and rubbings, scat, browsed plants, nests and burrows, gullies and runoff tracks, ground cover and foliage, and rock formations. Then he asked questions, pushing the students to put together the signs they had seen, to draw for themselves a recent and not-so-recent history of the plot of land:

> Look at the trees in the yard and the soil in the field and tell us whether the original settler carved his farm out of prairie or woods. Did he eat prairie chicken or wild turkey for his Thanksgiving? What plants grew here originally which do not grow here now? Why did they disappear? What did the prairie plants have to do with creating the corn-yielding capacity of this soil? Why does this soil erode now but not then?[2]

Leopold believed that "an ecologist often sees what is not there."[3] He made it seem like detective work: "The real game is decoding the messages

Robert A. McCabe family

*Leopold in his typical field attire at the Shack in 1937. No doubt there was a small notebook, a short pencil, and a knife for sharpening it in his pocket. One student noted: "The cane was not an aid in walking. It was a pointer . . . a prober, a clod-whacker; a tree, shrub, and flower investigator; and perhaps above all, a deadly threat to house cats wherever, whenever."[4] (Leopold disliked roaming pet cats because they preyed on wild birds unnecessarily, disturbing the natural ecosystem.)*

written on the face of the land."[5] He called the techniques of the observer "woodscraft, field skill, reading sign, sleuthing ability."[6] In his essay "Wherefore Wildlife Ecology?" he explained, "What I hope to teach is perhaps ecological research as an outdoor 'sport,' . . . amateur exploration, research for fun, in the field of the land."

Students learned to recognize trees by their silhouettes; to understand how glaciers affect landscapes and how soils affect plants; to explain which plants grow on northern slopes and which on southern ones and why; and to notice myriad other animal, plant, and soil relationships. Tests were usually composed of essay questions asking students to give examples of the interactions of nature they had observed.[7]

As for the Professor's graduate "wildlifers,"[8] they were as diverse in their research as the botany of a native prairie. Art Hawkins was studying game-management techniques; Doug Wade, the effects of drought on wildlife; Ellwood Moore, various grains for game food patches; Orville

The Aldo Leopold Foundation

*Leopold in the field with his students. This particular field was a residential area close to the university. Leopold did not have to go far to find nature to observe. He used his daily mile-long walks to and from the university to watch the interactions of species and note the subtle changes of the seasons: the first and last birds and blooms (firsts were much easier than lasts).*

*A slide Leopold used in class. He came upon this scene on a walk through Faville Grove. With no information but the visual, he theorized that this covey of quail died in a snow storm. They had gone to roost on the lee side of a grape tangle, where snow drifted over them, locking them in. They died in the circle formation typical of a covey roost. The slide is a good example of the types of things Leopold pointed out in the field and in his slide lectures.*

Lee, the movements of ring-necked pheasants; Irv Buss, the upland plover; Fred Hamerstrom, the prairie grouse; Fran Hamerstrom, dominance behavior in winter flocks of chickadees; Lyle Sowls, the Franklin ground squirrel and its relationship to nesting ducks; and Hans Albert Hochbaum, the canvasback duck.

In weekly conferences with his graduate students, Leopold went over every facet of the project under discussion—"good points, weak points, problems, anecdotes, future plans."[9] Leopold's students learned about more than wildlife; they found a personal role model in their professor, a well-esteemed professional who valued his family and "kindness." One student explained, "He treated his students with same consideration and respect as he did high ranking officials. . . . While you were with him, no one else had anything quite so important to discuss, or so you were made to feel."[10] Those who were not Leopold's students, however, were sometimes put off by his brusque, direct manner and the sureness with which he spoke. He showed no patience with anything petty or closed-minded, fake or materialistic.

Frances Hamerstrom, the nation's first female graduate student in wildlife management, received her degree from Leopold. "Aldo Leopold was the first professor I ever heard of to accept a girl graduate student," she said. "The very thought of a female wildlifer was so bizarre that it hardly bore consideration . . . [Yet] Aldo evaluated people—and was way ahead of his time in saying Nay to sex discrimination."[11]

When Leopold attended professional conferences or speaking engagements, he often brought one or two of his students with him. He nudged everyone he came in contact with, including his secretary, the spouses of his graduate students, and all his undergraduates, to become as involved in the field as possible.[12]

Leopold waged war on the artificial separation of studies and knowledge that occurs at schools and universities. His students were expected to read voraciously from a wide variety of sources dealing with their projects. He gave his reason, "In the classroom, the sciences seem to be separate. This is convenient for professors who have a hard enough time explaining even one science, but it doesn't help much in the field, where you invariably have to put sciences together to explain the simplest event."[13]

Leopold required intensive fieldwork, clear thinking on findings, and precise writing from his graduate students. After handing in a paper, most lived in utter dread of getting it back. Especially disheartening was a wavy vertical line in the margin or the word "wormy."[14] One student explained, "He taught us that 'muddy writing' is caused by 'muddy thinking' or vice versa."[15] Another remembered that "he was generous with praise when he could be,"[16] but the Professor would often make a "blizzard of blue marks" across your paper—and then sit side by side with you to advise and encourage. Most students suffered through a multitude of drafts before Leopold was satisfied that a paper was ready to be published. He explained the process to one of his students:

> Think of it this way. In spite of all the advances of modern science, it still takes seven waters to clean spinach for the pot. . . . And for all my writings to this day, it still takes seven editings, sometimes seventeen, before I let it go off to press. Remember that. We're all in the same boat.[17]

And they were. Leopold scribbled over and over each of his drafts, then let them sit for awhile in his "cooler"—a large portfolio of embossed leather bulging with manuscripts, packed away in the right-hand corner of his large Leopold Desk. "Here's where I put my stuff to simmer," he told the student. "It doesn't change in there, but I do. When I get an idea or a new slant or a fresh view, why, hell, it's right there where I can grab it."[18]

By the late 1930s, grad students were wandering into the basement of the Soils Building at nearly any hour to tally research results, consult with the Professor, dissect specimens, or identify plants in the makeshift laboratory. One student had his office in the hall on a seed drill, and another on a John Deere sower.

In the spring of 1938, a university review committee set up a series of meetings to decide if the game-management program should continue to be funded. The Professor's dedicated band of students had no doubts. One spring evening, the gallant group slipped into the Soils Building and loaded up the furniture, laboratory, files, paintings, and books. One student stood guard while the rest moved the entire Division of Game Management to a rundown Victorian house by the railroad tracks. They canvassed their own homes and apartments for extra furniture so they could "take possession" of the whole first floor.

When the Professor showed up at the Soils Building the next morning, nothing remained of his former office. His students led him to the porch of 424 University Farm Place. The once-elegant building had been the family home of the dean of the College of Agriculture before it was given to the university.

Leopold was greeted by a large, L-shaped room, complete with a marble fireplace, a small foyer for student conferences, and Vivian Horn sitting contentedly at her oak desk as if she had always been there. Behind her desk, a door opened into his new office and library. There stood his Leopold Desk with pipe and ashtray all in place, and next to them, a Mason jar with flowers. To the back of the building was a kitchen that would also serve as a laboratory, and a small room that had been converted into a darkroom. A grand oak stairway, somewhat the worse for wear, led up to a third-floor, half-story attic, where the students could study or socialize. State and federal agencies inhabited the second floor and basement.

The "new" quarters took Leopold by surprise. When he called university authorities to tell them his office had moved, they informed

Robert A. McCabe family

*424 University Farm Place (in its heyday, years before it became home to the Department of Wildlife Management). Each day, Leopold arrived a few hours before Vivian to catch up on his voluminous reading and work on one of his journal articles before the students arrived. At lunch, he took a break and walked home to eat with Estella. After a short nap, he'd be back at work.*

him that those rooms had been assigned to others, and he could not have them. He replied that, in fact, he already did have them, for better or for worse, and he hung up. Then he leaned back in his chair, looked at his students in a slightly bewildered way, and smiled.

The division had found a home. As one of the Professor's students wrote, "The old house fitted him like a well-worn hunting coat."[19] The Wisconsin Alumni Research Foundation made it official by providing funds for Leopold's program for another year. But it would still be up to the state legislature to make the decision permanent.

Within a few weeks, unidentifiable smells wafted from the kitchen/dissecting laboratory, the multitude of books and journals Leopold had collected filled the bookshelves, and the oval mahogany table in the foyer hosted lively discussions. Students periodically checked in with Vivian to see if the Professor was available; if he leaned back in his chair when they knocked, he was ready to chat—otherwise, he would appoint a mutually convenient time. Every other Monday night, the graduate students gathered in the third-floor party room for a seminar. The topics, presented by guest speakers and research students, ranged from "The Need of a Life History of Ragweed" to "The 1937 Nesting Census Study" to "Game Management Objectives in Relation to Agronomy."

"Those seminars were so powerful," Frederick Hamerstrom remarked, "because you either had it or you didn't have it. And if you didn't have it—POW! . . . then you were wide, wide open, and you got it!"[20] The group would fire questions at the presenter and race into discussions that lasted late into the evening. Vivian Horn, Estella, the students' spouses, and varying members of the Leopold clan were regular attendees at these evening seminars. The discussions were lightened by apples and, occasionally, beer. When Leopold passed a wastebasket for the cores, everyone knew it was time to go home.

Though the rest of the Professor's evenings were reserved for his family, the Leopolds often invited students and friends to potlucks, Sunday picnics, and fall hunting weekends at the Shack. Visitors came to expect Aldo to retire early, leaving Estella to preside over the rest of the evening cordialities. Estella was definitely the more social of the two; she usually had to convince Aldo to attend a party or movie. Invariably, he would be glad he went.

The couple even won a faculty dance contest or two.

When students went with the Professor to his home, on hunting trips, or out into the field with him on research projects, they often got to see more intimate or rougher sides of him. One wildlifer, James B. Hale, recalls the time he saw the "frontier" side of Leopold when he fell waist-deep into very cold water during a midwinter pheasant count at the Arboretum: "The dunking was followed immediately by about 10 seconds of heart felt and unprintable curses by the Professor, to the astonishment of the non-plussed onlookers. . . . I think the episode helped us grad students gain a better opinion of the Professor's humanity. Anyone who could cuss like that deserved our respect."[21]

In the fall of 1938, as classes were about to begin, Leopold made changes to his curriculum. Game Management 118 became Wildlife Ecology 118 (a course still suited to both majors and nonmajors). His focus had shifted permanently from game management to living harmoniously with the land and its wildlife.

With his time stretched between his university activities, obligations to national organizations, a writing career, and home, Aldo's health began to unravel. He endured severe headaches, and his eyes started to bother him, as they had when he was in college.

The Shack proved his closest and dearest escape. On Friday afternoons, while he waited for everyone to pack, Aldo clipped the hedge. No one misunderstood—it was time to head out.

The Leopolds had chinked the Shack's walls, added a lean-to, and extended the chimney. Vivian Horn commented on this ongoing labor: "This family seemed to think it was a lot of fun to spend a vacation together doing the hardest kind of work."[22] The cohesion of the Leopolds' enjoyment of the Shack struck her. "In many families, the children seem to find their pleasures and interests away from home, but with the Leopolds it was different. I used to notice that frequently the children preferred going to the Shack to some other activity."[23]

Each season engendered new activities. Spring planting passed into wildflower tending, fishing, swimming, and canoeing. Fall colors called the family to pheasant and duck hunting and long bird-watching walks. The frozen days of winter demanded cross-country travel on skis and the cutting of firewood. The Leopolds fed winged winter residents and caught them in homemade traps in order to band them. One plucky chickadee, #65290, returned to them four years running.

In the middle of February 1939, the family arrived at the Shack to find it had been ransacked. Broken plates and benches lay strewn about.

The Aldo Leopold Foundation

*The Leopold family at the Shack in about 1940: (top) Aldo, Estella, Luna, Starker; (bottom) Nina, Estella, Jr., Gus. Carl took the photograph. Estella usually brought huge batches of corn bread swathed in honey along on Shack weekends to keep the work crews full and content.*

An axe was wedged into the fireplace mantle, and kerosene had been tossed over Estella's shattered jars of jams and honey. Nina recalled that each member of the family "just went into a corner and began to cry. All, that is, but Dad. He just looked around, saw our state, and burst into a big smile. 'I didn't know how much this place meant to you,' he said. 'Let's get busy.'"[24]

They cleaned the place up, whitewashed the walls, and added a wooden floor while they were at it. Then they watched for the signs of spring.

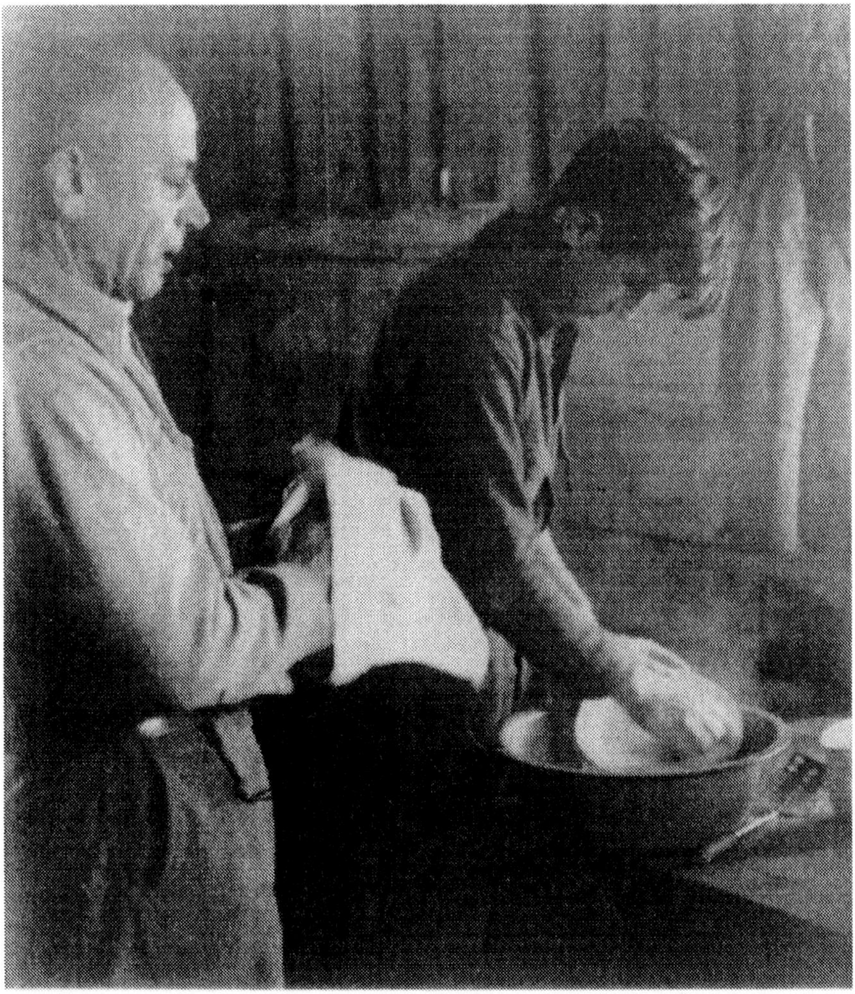
The Aldo Leopold Foundation

*Aldo and the kids would take over the cooking and cleaning at the Shack so Estella could take a break.*

(Later they found out some teenage boys had done the damage for fun.)

As spring unfolded, notes in the Shack journal described the budding of the pines, the blooming of the first trillium, the return of the geese, the winnowing (territorial call) of the snipes, the planting of trees. On warm nights in April and May, just before sunset, two or three members of the family would sneak off to a mossy open spot in the woods to wait for the "sky-dance theater":

> Knowing the place and the hour, you seat yourself under a bush to the east of the dance floor and wait, watching against the sunset for the woodcock's arrival. He flies in low from some neighboring thicket, alights on the bare moss, and at once begins the overture: a series of queer throaty peents [nasal calls] spaced about two seconds apart. . . . Suddenly the peenting ceases and the bird flutters skyward in a series of wide spirals, emitting a musical twitter. Up and up he goes, the spirals steeper and smaller, the twittering louder and louder, until the performer is only a speck in the sky. Then, without warning, he tumbles like a crippled plane. . . . At a few feet from the ground he levels off and returns to the peenting ground, usually to the exact spot where the performance began, and there resumes his peenting.[25]

After an invigorating weekend at the Shack, the family would hurry home to be in time for the Ford Radio hour, which Aldo particularly enjoyed. Nina recalled, "Dad would sit and hold my hand, and the tears would roll down my face, he was so warm. You just felt like there wasn't anything like it."[26]

In the spring of 1939, as the school year finished, Leopold waited to hear if his contract would be renewed. Leopold's friends and colleagues wrote to state legislators, urging them to make his position permanent. Ding Darling described Leopold's national reputation: "Aldo Leopold is recognized in every circle of conservationists as the ranking authority and leading voice in the country. His voluntary contributions to the conservation literature of the country are standards by which all lesser authorities are judged."[27]

Word finally came. Not only had the state granted Leopold the funds to continue, they had given him his own department—the Department of Wildlife Management in the College of Agriculture.

# Paths of Violence

# 1939-1945

*Harmony with land is like harmony with a friend;*
*you cannot cherish his right hand and chop off his left. . . .*
*you cannot love game and hate predators;*
*you cannot conserve the waters and waste the ranges;*
*you cannot build the forest and mine the farm.*
*The land is one organism.*

*"The Round River,"* Round River

In September 1939, Germany invaded Poland. During the dark months of 1939, 1940, and 1941, Europe exploded with tanks, bombs, and guns. The violent side of Hitler's new German policies proved worse than Leopold had imagined possible.

A letter arrived from Leopold's host in Germany, Alfred Schottlaender. Schottlaender's wife had turned him in to the secret police for making anti-Hitler comments. He had been interned both at Dachau and Buchenwald, but had managed to escape to Kenya. He was writing to ask Aldo to help his brother, who was still in Germany.

Leopold contacted those he knew, and a place was found in South Africa for Alfred's brother. "My dear friend Leopold," responded Alfred, "[You] have given me back the faith of faithfulness, truth, and friendship still existing on earth, which I nearly had lost after having lived to see such terrible disappointments in my own country which I loved so much and served all my life."[1]

Violence seemed to be the common link between the many ways

University of Wisconsin-Madison Archives X25 2947

*Carl in U.S. Marine's uniform. Stationed in the Pacific during the war, Carl was not allowed to tell his family where he was. After reading one long-awaited letter, Aldo turned to Estella excitedly, "I know where Carl is! I know where Carl is!"[2] He had pinpointed his son's location on a Pacific island from Carl's description of the birds.*

humans acted toward the land and toward each other. Leopold began to refer to conservation as a movement toward "nonviolent land use," where changes are made gradually and carefully, keeping the land community stable.

Then the exploding violence hit the States: the Japanese attacked Pearl Harbor on December 7, 1941. The next day, Carl enlisted in the marines. On the edge of twenty-two, he had just begun graduate studies in wildlife ecology in Missouri. He hurried to marry Keena Rogers before leaving for combat. Luna enlisted in the army and was sent to California as an army engineer. Starker, who had married and was expecting a child, kept working, dreading the mail, which could carry a draft notice any day.

Many of the Professor's graduate and undergraduate students quit school to enlist. Vivian Horn resigned to do her part for the war effort.

Sometime in 1942, a round robin of letters was begun between the department and those who had left. Each recipient added comments and sent the letter on to someone else. Many of the letters were filled with jottings on wildlife research conducted at faraway ports and stations. One former student kept track of the migrating birds that stopped to rest on his ship. Another wrote: "I wish to close with a wish and a prayer, that when this is over every one of us will again be sitting shoulder to shoulder at the Professor's table 'swapping yarns.'"[3]

During the war, Aldo and his two Estellas became a quiet threesome. Nina had married a zoology student, Bill Elder, in September 1941, leaving fifteen-year-old Estella alone with her parents at home. They waited tensely for the sporadic letters Carl sent from the Pacific and saved gas-rationing coupons for trips to the Shack.

Most days at the Shack, Aldo woke hours before dawn, around 3:30 or 4:00 A.M., to make coffee and take his seat outside on the homemade bench to do his personal wildlife research. He'd listen for the first twitters,

The Aldo Leopold Foundation

*Aldo writing in his journal at the Shack. "With such dignity as I can muster of a July morning, I step from my cabin door, bearing in either hand my emblems of sovereignty: a coffeepot and notebook. I seat myself on a bench, facing the white wake of the morning star. . . . I get out my watch, pour my coffee, and lay my notebook on my knee. This is the cue for the proclamations to begin."*[4]

cackles, and calls as they rose in intensity with the sunlight, which he tracked with a light meter. Then, in the Shack journal, he'd note the light-meter reading taken at the time of each song.

Every spring since 1937, Aldo had also kept track of the first buds, blooms, and arrivals of migrating species at the Shack. These phenological records had grown in detail with each season, until finally, Leopold assembled them for publication with the findings of a botany student, Sara Elizabeth (Libbie) Jones. In their article, Leopold explained the pleasure and interest of such records:

> Many of the events of the annual cycle recur year after year, in a regular order. A year-to-year record of this order is a record of the rates at which solar energy flows to and through living things. These are the arteries of the land. By tracing their responses to the sun, phenology may eventually shed some light on the ultimate enigma, the land's inner workings.[5]

Aldo's interest in phenology did little to distract him from his mounting responsibilities. As the brutality of the war increased, Leopold became entangled in vehement debates on the conservation front. Both state and national governments were promoting the construction of dams for more power and the clearcutting of wilderness areas and state forests for more timber and roads. Leopold fought these acts of violence against nature with his sharpened pencil and lined pads. His words deepened in philosophical content and scientific scope. As one student said:

> When most biologists were thinking of individuals, he was thinking in terms of populations. When it was usual to think of populations . . . he was thinking of ecosystems, and of humans as components of ecosystems. . . . He was seeing beyond the preservation of nature apart—toward the integration of human and natural worlds.[6]

The titles of some of his most significant addresses, lectures, and essays of the war years show the depth of the human questions he was tackling:

"Economics, Philosophy, and Land," "A Biotic View of Land," "War Ecology," "Land Use and Democracy," "Wildlife in American Culture," "The Role of Wildlife in a Liberal Education," "A Conservation Esthetic." His solutions to conservation problems emphasized widespread, in-depth ecological education to change American assumptions about the land and the society's cultural values. He wrote, "The real substance of conservation lies not in the physical projects of the government, but in the mental processes of citizens. . . . All the acts of government, in short, are of slight importance to conservation except as they affect the acts and thoughts of citizens."[7]

Leopold had a chance to distill this theoretical principle into action as he became embroiled in state politics. Since 1936, reports had been coming in of a population explosion in Wisconsin's white-tailed deer herds. The state had been nearly wolfless for years, due to an effective bounty system. Just as on the Kaibab Plateau, the deer were destroying their habitat: they were feeding on the seedlings of the state's newly replanted forests, and many were starving to death.

At first, Wisconsinites refused to acknowledge the problem. Less than twenty years ago, the conservationists had pressed for hunting limits and wolf elimination, saying there were too few deer. Now there were too many deer. Why should they believe the conservationists?

In 1942, as the deer crisis was coming to a head, the governor called upon Leopold to serve on the Conservation Commission, which appointed him to its Citizens' Deer Committee. (Shortly thereafter, the Wisconsin Academy invited Leopold to lead a new Committee on Natural Resources. This group was also concerned about the deer situation.) A friend, Wallace Grange, wrote of the governor's decision:

> I am still rubbing my eyes in disbelief over the state's inconceivably good fortune in having you on the Commission. I thought those things happened only in the storybooks. . . . The situation had become so hopeless as to be almost irremediable. Now it is as fresh as a seed which has germinated after long dormancy. . . . The ecology of the Conservation Commission has been subjected to something that will leave its mark on the face of things from here onward.[8]

The *State Journal* applauded the appointment just as enthusiastically.

> Aldo Leopold may not be a popular commissioner with everyone. He, better than any other man in Wisconsin and probably better than any other man in the entire country, knows what real conservation is and how to achieve it. That will involve stepping on toes, but, fortified by an informed love for nature and having no political axes to grind, he will not be reluctant to step. . . . If the people of Wisconsin allow men like Leopold to direct their conservation program, the generations to come will be blessed.[9]

The *Journal*'s words proved prophetic.

Leopold's public education effort began without delay. He led members of the public into winter fields. There, they saw fawns too weak to stand and does that could not flee when people approached. Leopold called their attention to seedlings, limbs, and young trunks that had been nibbled to nothing. The state Conservation Department supported his teaching by producing a documentary film entitled "Starvation Stalks the Deer" explaining (and, in Leopold's opinion, sensationalizing) the situation. A lot of people were swayed, but not enough; changing years of thinking was a difficult task. "The real problem is not how we handle the deer in this emergency,"[10] Leopold told Gordon MacQuarrie, an outdoors writer for the *Milwaukee Journal*. "The real problem is one of human management." Leopold later theorized:

> This public we are talking about consists of three groups. Group 1 is the largest; it is indifferent to conservation questions. Group 2 is the smallest; it thinks with its head, but is silent. Group 3 is of intermediate size, and does all its thinking with mouth or pen. Perhaps a Conservation Commission would do better not to try to convert Group 3, but to convince Group 2 that there is an issue, and that it should say or do something about it. Perhaps this would shorten the 23 years. [It had taken that long to get an effective conservation policy passed.][11]

In the winter of 1942-43, the situation became critical. Something had to be done immediately to reduce the number of deer and save the forests. Leopold advised the state policymakers on the Conservation Commission that hunters be allowed to shoot does rather than bucks; this would bring herd numbers down quickly and improve the sex ratio. Overbrowsed refuges had to be opened to hunting, with increased bag limits in areas with higher herd populations. He warned, however, that intense hunting would only be a short-term solution. Hunting could never approach the natural efficiency of predation. As proof, he cited the deer population eruptions in other predatorless states. Thus, the state must abolish the bounty on wolves and encourage a small population of wolves in the wilder regions of the state.

The commission made what it considered a compromise with the Professor. It instituted a short buck season and a longer doe season to be enforced consistently throughout the state, and it put a ban on wolf bounties.

Leopold saw this as the worst of all possible solutions. Indeed, the compromise turned out to be a disaster. It became known as "the crime of '43."[12] During that year's hunting season, deer were slaughtered in easy-to-reach areas, while herd numbers remained large in more remote spots. Poaching was rife.

Enraged citizens called for an end to advice from wildlife managers and a return of the wolf bounty. Leopold stood firm against the tide. He asked for a study on the ecology of the wolf in Wisconsin so the public would have definite facts upon which to base its decision. But the prejudice against the wolf ran too deep to be undone by science. One sporting club couched its rage in racist wartime metaphors:

> The wolf is the Nazi of the forest. He takes the deer and some small fry. The fox is the sly Jap who takes the choice morsels of game and the song birds. Can Professor Leopold justify their existence because deer meant for human consumption should be fed to the Nazi because we must have that protection for the trees?[13]

The venom of the attacks increased. Some hunters in Hayward, Wisconsin, started the "Save the Deer Club." They assailed Leopold and the commission in their newsletter, calling him "Bambi killer."[14] He had said publicly, "Those who assume that we would be better off without any wolves are assuming more knowledge of how nature works than I can claim to possess."[15] The club newsletter retaliated, "Read it again because it has that touch of 'Leopoldian egotism' and insinuates that he, the great Aldo, places his knowledge above that of any Wisconsin citizen."[16]

The deer controversy unraveled Leopold's health even more. Pains in his thighs and upper jaw required surgery. Sleep eluded him.

The strain on him showed itself in other areas as well. Leopold found himself painfully at odds with some of his colleagues and former students. Hans Albert Hochbaum, a former student skilled in wildlife research and art, was doing pioneering work at the Delta Duck Station in Manitoba. Leopold had helped establish the waterfowl research center in 1937. A report required for additional funding divided the two men—Leopold preferred a short, clear, objective summary; Hochbaum wanted a descriptive book with sketches that would draw readers into the life of the marsh before explaining the research accomplishments. The further they progressed into the project, the more their approaches clashed.

Misunderstandings and hard feelings escalated as the clock ticked, and the project was delayed again and again. Working through the mail intensified the gaps. The Professor finally decided to back off and let his fledgling fly on his own. He resigned from the project, and Hochbaum was set up as the station director with Leopold's approval. This move saved their friendship and gave Hochbaum the freedom and confidence he needed to finish the report in his own way and on his own schedule. It evolved into a book called *Canvasback on a Prairie Marsh*. When it was published, Leopold wrote Hochbaum, "I can't help but swell up with pride about the book."[17] The book won two awards: the Brewster Medal of the American Ornithologists' Union and the 1944 Literary Award of the Wildlife Society. "'Congratulations' seems a mild term for my sentiments," Leopold told his former student.[18]

A similar disagreement arose with Paul Errington, a scientist working with Leopold on prairie-chicken research. When they came to a standoff on interpretations, management philosophies, and conclusions, Leopold again withdrew from the project. Serious discussions, and at times disagreements, came with the research territory as surely as explosions with deep mining. Yet many of Leopold's colleagues and students recall that the Professor hardly ever ended tense conversations without the statement: "Let's not sweat the small potatoes."

Joan Hochbaum

*Aldo Leopold with Hans Albert Hochbaum at the Delta Duck Station.*

In the early 1940s, Leopold's responsibilities at the university lightened. The student population was low because of the war, and the Professor had hired a former student, Robert McCabe, as the department assistant. Leopold was able to put in double time on his writing, reworking research notes, articles, speeches, passages from his hunting notebooks, and entries from the Shack journals for a book of personal essays.

In a strange turnabout, Albert Hochbaum acted as Leopold's editor for the book project. Leopold had asked Hochbaum to prepare sketches to accompany the text, so as Aldo finished each piece, he sent it off to Albert at the Delta Duck Station. Albert's comments cut to the heart of the writings. The pieces were beautifully descriptive, he assessed, but they lacked something: humility. "You never drop a hint that you yourself have once despoiled [the land], or at least had a strong hand in it," Albert wrote. "You'll have to admit you've got at least a drop of blood on your hands."[19] He later added, "I think your case for the wilderness is all the stronger if, in one of these pieces, you admit that you haven't always smoked the same tobacco."[20]

Aldo did not immediately agree. He thought Albert's suggestions might take him off on a tangent and ruin the focus of his book. But Albert pressed him. "It is only by accepting ourselves for what we are, the best of

University of Wisconsin-Madison Archives X25 682

*Robert McCabe, Flick, and Aldo after a woodcock hunt.*

University of Wisconsin-Madison Archives (photo by Robert McCabe) X2 194N

*For Leopold, hunting was both a scientific experience and a recreational one. In the field, he usually recorded in his hunting journal the sex, age, and weight of his catch as well as the contents of its gullet or scat. He made this note on a quail he encountered: "One cock flew into elm and defecated on my face: could identify blackberry skins in droppings."*[21]

us and the worst of us, that we can hold any hope for the future."[22]

Aldo thanked him, stating that these were the most valuable comments he had received from anyone on these essays. Albert dashed off one more letter on the subject: Aldo's unique gift was not that he was "an inspired genius," he said, but that he was like "any other ordinary fellow trying to put two and two together." The Professor simply "added up his sums better than most."[23] Wrong trails taken were as important as right ones.

On April 1, 1944, in response to Albert's comments and his own wranglings with the Conservation Commission, Leopold wrote the essay, "Thinking Like a Mountain." In it, he described the mother wolf that he had shot in the Apache National Forest; he told of the fierce green fire he had seen in her dying eyes.

> I was young then, and full of trigger-itch. I thought that because fewer wolves meant more deer, that no wolves would mean hunters' paradise. But after seeing the green fire die, I sensed that neither the wolf nor the mountain agreed with such a view.[24]

Leopold concluded the essay by referring to the words of Thoreau: "'In wildness is the preservation of the world.'[25] Perhaps this is the hidden meaning in the howl of the wolf, long known among the mountains, but seldom perceived among men." Hochbaum thought the essay fit the bill perfectly.

The wolf became a symbol for Leopold of "the fierce green fire" of healthy, wild land. Those who understand the role of predators understand some of the inner workings and drama of the land itself. "You cannot love game and hate predators. . . . The land is one organism."[26]

Leopold's shift in philosophy toward predators in the animal kingdom applied to the plant kingdom as well. Leopold once considered fire the forest and grasslands' greatest enemy. Now he began experimenting with it as one of the elements that could help move degraded land toward greater health. At the arboretum, Leopold and his students worked with botanist John Curtis in setting up small burn plots aimed at uncovering the role of fire in prairie growth cycles. True to their suspicions, the scientists discovered fire was an essential ingredient in a healthy ecosystem. It rebuilt

University of Wisconsin-Madison Arboretum

*Leopold, second from left, works with students to burn a section of restored prairie at the arboretum. The students are Pepper Jackson to the Professor's left, James Hale, and Elizabeth Jones.*

the soil, diversified plant and animal life, and broke open the seeds of some plant species.

Over the summer of 1944, Leopold wrote, rewrote, rearranged, and added to his essays before sending them to various publishers. Publishers Knopf and Macmillan had both shown interest in the book as it evolved. Then Macmillan rejected the reworked manuscript, and Knopf asked for major changes and additions. With Hochbaum's help, Leopold went through the painful process of sorting through the comments.

He had no respite from his other ordeals. The battles over the deer and wolf continued with Leopold as the public's favorite target. For many years to come, Wisconsinites would have to grapple with the issue, and inevitably, Leopold would be caught in the crossfire. Mercilessly, the war and its deadly machinery also sped dangerously onward. On Christmas Day, 1944, Aldo wrote to Starker, "The war has us all worried. Not so good. Love to you all, AL."[27]

Out of the blue, in February 1945, Carl called from Chicago to say that he had just arrived home on a month's leave. He and his wife Keena

*This slide, taken by Leopold in 1944 at the arboretum, illustrated for Leopold's classes the importance of fire in the ecology of a prairie. The big bluestem on the left grew after a burn; the bluestem on the right had not experienced fire. Nina stands between to give perspective.*

took the train to Madison a few days later. Carl stepped off the train, and Aldo and Estella wrapped their son in their arms. For the first time, Carl saw his father cry.

Then, in August of 1945, after a horrendous crescendo, the war ended. All of Leopold's graduate students returned to the states unharmed, but two of his undergraduates had been killed in action. Pondering these deaths and the agonies of the atomic bomb, Leopold sat down to write an essay he never finished:

> We are now confronted by the fact . . . that wars are no longer won; . . . all wars are lost by all who wage them; the only difference between participants is the degree and kind of losses they sustain. . . . Science has so sharpened the fighter's sword that it is impossible for him to cut his enemy without cutting himself.[28]

# GREAT POSSESSIONS 1945-1948

*When we see land as a community to which we belong, we may begin to use it with love and respect.*

*Foreword,* A Sand County Almanac

Soldiers returning from the war who longed to be a part of something life-affirming and "pure" rushed into the ranks of the wildlife profession. In the fall of 1945 and spring of 1946, the Professor's classes were packed beyond his abilities to teach. He had to turn some students away. He relied more on Robert McCabe, sought additional assistants, and tried to reduce his outside commitments. But his national stature had grown to the point where he could not turn away some recognition and its attendant duties. He was elected honorary vice-president of the American Forestry Association and president of the Ecological Society of America.

Periodically, with increasing frequency and fury, pains exploded on the left side of Aldo's face. It was like "somebody rising suddenly from behind a bush and bashing you with a sledgehammer."[1] The pain would stop him in mid-sentence. He had to shut his eyes and put pressure on the side of his face until the pain passed. Doctors diagnosed it as tic douloureux, or facial neuralgia, a swelling around one of the main facial nerves. They didn't know what caused it or what to do about it. Aldo decided to wait and see if a summer's ease at home and at the Shack would erase the pain and make surgery unnecessary.

Ten years of work and affectionate tending had radically changed the landscape of the Shack. Nearly thirty thousand trees and shrubs thrived in patterns that were both random (never in rows) and intentional (the patches of flora fit the soils and the curves of the landscape). Overgrowth hid the river from view, pines defined parts of the land, and the experimental prairie had taken hold.

University of Wisconsin-Madison Archives (photo by Robert McCabe)

*Leopold in 1946 measuring the growth of the pines planted at the Shack. He once wrote: "The only conclusion I have ever reached about trees is that I love all trees, but I am in love with pines."[2] (The pinery at the University of Wisconsin Arboretum is called the "Aldo Leopold Pines.")*

Bruce Carl Leopold

*Like grandfather, like grandson. Aldo watches as Bruce Carl Leopold strikes a pose with his pipe at 2222 Van Hise.*

As young Estella's studies and social life began to envelop her, Aldo and Estella went to the Shack more and more as a twosome. Grandparents now, the Leopolds did get to babysit Bruce Carl Leopold that summer—the eldest child of Luna and his wife, Carolyn Clugston Leopold. For part of the time they took him to the Shack, and, as always, Aldo was able to relax, and his pains were somewhat relieved.

Other burdens could not be eased. The deer problem and several state conservation issues persisted. Now at the age of sixty, Leopold had attained such national and international fame that he was consulted on almost every major conservation issue. Yet his belief in political solutions was nebulous; he was more convinced than ever that people had to assume a code of ethics and cultural values that would entail new political perspectives and individual actions. "No important change in ethics was ever accomplished without an internal change in our intellectual emphasis, loyalties, affections, and convictions," he wrote. "In our attempt to make conservation easy, we have made it trivial."[3] Conservation would not be achieved "until the Landowner changes his ways of using land, and he in turn cannot change his ways until his teachers, bankers, customers, editors, governors, and trespassers change their ideas about what land is for. To change ideas about what land is for is to change ideas about what anything is for."[4]

Americans would have to develop an "ecological conscience" and acknowledge they are simply members of the land community. To achieve this, they would have to expand their code of decency, honor, respect, and responsibility to include the natural world. "Ecology is the science of communities," Leopold said, "and the ecological conscience is therefore the ethics of community life. . . . An ecological conscience, then, is an affair of the mind as well as the heart."[5]

Leopold took the risk of defining an ecological standard of morality in his address "The Ecological Conscience:" "A thing is right only when it tends to preserve the integrity, stability, and beauty of the community, and the community includes the soil, waters, fauna, and flora, as well as people."[6] He later refined the wording, replacing "community" with "biotic community"[7] and adding the essential counterpart: "[A thing] is wrong when it tends otherwise."[8] He dubbed his definition: "The Land Ethic."

How could such a revolution in cultural thought be accomplished? For Leopold, "Ethics are a kind of community-instinct-in-the-making."[9] He told his students:

> If the individual has a warm personal understanding of land, he will perceive of his own accord that it is something more than a

> breadbasket. He will see land as a community of which he is only a member, albeit now the dominant one. He will see the beauty, as well as the utility, of the whole, and know the two cannot be separated. We love (and make intelligent use of) what we have learned to understand.[10]

In answer to his own question, "Who is the land?" Leopold responded, "We are, but no less the meanest flower that blows. Land ecology at the outset discards the fallacious notion that the wild community is one thing, the human community another."[11]

Though he talked of morality and ethics, Leopold rarely mentioned religion. His parents had been Lutherans, but did not often attend church. As an adult, Aldo had been to church for his own wedding and for Nina's—not often beyond that, though Estella remained a practicing Catholic all her life (when the family was at the Shack, however, she did not leave to go to mass). On a few occasions, Leopold hinted that churches, if they chose to, could play a strong role in hastening the integration of a land ethic into the cultural code of morals.

Aldo told his daughter Estella that "he thought organized religion was all right for many people, but did not partake of it himself."[12] He believed "there was a mystical supreme power that guided the Universe, but to him this power was not a personal God. It was more akin to the laws of nature."[13] Thus, his view of ethics did not necessitate a defined concept of God; nor did it preclude it.

By the spring of 1947, the pain in Aldo's face had grown so severe that he received an injection of alcohol directly into the nerve to deaden it. This appeared to work at first. Over the summer's respite from pain, he organized his writings into three sections. The first—"A Sauk County Almanac"—contained seasonal and historical descriptions of the land around the Shack in calendar order. The second—"Sketches Here and There"—encompassed articles on places more distant and the conservation lessons learned there. The third section—"The Upshot"—held his conclusions about land, history, ethics, and wilderness. This final grouping was constructed from some of Leopold's latest and most significant addresses and articles. Together, they formed the power station of his philosophical summations. With his foreword, Leopold wove the three sections into a coherent whole under the title "Great Possessions" and sent the manuscript to Knopf on September 11, 1947.

As Leopold was finishing the project, his facial spasms came back with a vengeance. His doctor requested that he spend August in bed. All his children came to see him during that time, and on September 19, Minnesota's Mayo Clinic admitted him for surgery. A hole was cut behind

Robert A. McCabe family (photo by Aldo Leopold)

*Classroom slide of a skunk track in the snow at the Shack. The opening of Leopold's book of essays may have been based on this sighting: "Each year . . . there comes a night of thaw when the tinkle of dripping water is heard on the land. It brings strange stirrings, not only to creatures abed for the night, but to some who have been asleep for the winter. The hibernating skunk, curled up in his deep den, uncurls himself and ventures forth to prowl the wet world, dragging his belly in the snow. His track marks one of the earliest datable events in the cycle of beginnings and ceasings which we call a year."*[14]

his left ear, and the main nerve snipped. After the operation, the left side of Leopold's face drooped; he no longer had any feeling there. He began to have trouble focusing his thoughts and remembering names.

By October, Leopold was back at home, work, and the Shack. He had to sit out the hunting season in a portable canvas chair, watching others. His concentration and memory improved, but he often needed prompting from Bob McCabe. Because his tongue was still constricted and he had lost nerve control, Aldo worried that he was mumbling and slurring his words. Nearly every day, he asked Estella, "How does it sound to you, dear?"[15] She tried to reassure him his speech was fine, but to little avail.

In November, Leopold received a letter from Knopf suggesting that he rewrite the entire book, deleting sections two and three. The blow was too strong.

Luna stepped in. He stated that his father was too "softhearted to deal with these people,"[16] and that he would handle the book negotiations from then on. Aldo readily agreed to let Luna "get [him] off the hook."[17]

*University of Wisconsin-Madison Archives (photo by Robert McCabe) X2 191*

*Some of the Professor's graduate students join him for a working retreat at the Shack in 1947. Left to right: Bruce S. Wright, Donald R. Thompson, Leopold, James R. Beer, Steven Richards, and Clifford Bakkom (kneeling).*

Since Albert Hochbaum was too busy to do the sketches, Luna made a deal with a new illustrator, Charles Schwartz. Then Luna consulted with an editor at Oxford University Press who sounded interested. On December 19, 1947, Leopold mailed copies of the manuscript—dedicated to "My Estella"—to Oxford and to a press in New York.

Aldo's eyes began to dry and blur. He had to use special drops to keep them wet. At the university, Bob McCabe helped him apply the drops, while he guarded carefully the Professor's time and energy. Leopold trudged on with classes, meetings, field visits, arboretum work, and writing.

On January 11, 1948, Leopold turned sixty-one. The next day he attended a commissioners' meeting, fighting dam-building projects on Wisconsin's few remaining wild rivers.

His eyes did not heal, and he had to return to the Mayo Clinic for another surgery. He endured the rest of February with an eye patch.

At the end of the month, the federal government asked if Leopold would be one of the United States' representatives at a United Nations-sponsored conference on conservation in 1949. Leopold had reached the pinnacle of his career.

As his eyes gradually healed, he eased back into his duties. On Wednesday, April 14, he received word from Oxford University Press—they wanted to publish his book. He was ecstatic. Estella, Jr., said it made him "a little more at ease, feeling better about life."[18]

That Friday, Aldo, his two Estellas, and young Estella's boyfriend packed up supplies for spring break at the Shack. Aldo was still a bit weak, and he tired easily, but he was more cheerful than he had been in a long time. Estella's friend left Sunday night, and the next morning, the family began its work in the pleasantest of ways. Estella, Jr., wrote:

> Monday, we three drove in for the pines at Baraboo and walked around the Shack while Daddy showed us the blooming pasque flowers and Hepatica with great pride. We made a special trip to the clay hill, Dad and Mom arm in arm, so Dad could show us a 'surprise'—a single Dentaria plant he had found.[19]

Tuesday, they planted their trees. About 10:30 Wednesday morning, the Leopolds spotted smoke coming from a neighbor's farm. The wind was blowing the fire eastward, in their direction. Aldo sent young Estella for the fire pump and her mother for buckets. He grabbed a sprinkling can, and they gathered up coats and gloves, a gunnysack, a broom, and a shovel.

They loaded the car with filled buckets and drove to where they could see flames. The elder Estella, armed with a wet gunny sack and a broom, patrolled the nearby marsh to keep sparks from crossing the road. Aldo and young Estella hurried on to fight the blaze at close range. Other neighbors arrived to pitch in.

Aldo sent his daughter to a neighbor's house to call the Fire Department and the Wildlife Conservation Department. He stayed to wet the grasses with the water pump.

Shortly after she left, Aldo's chest tightened in pain. He pulled the pump off his back and sat down to rest. Putting his head on a clump of grass, he folded his arms over his chest. The attack did not go away. Aldo Leopold died of a heart attack before anyone knew he was in trouble. The fire passed lightly over him.

As the flames died down, young Estella saw a neighbor coming toward her from the area where she had left her dad. She sensed almost at once what he was going to say.

# Afterword

*I am trying to teach you that this alphabet of "natural objects"*
*(soils and rivers, birds and beasts)*
*spells out a story. . . .*
*Once you learn how to read the land,*
*I have no fear of what you will do to it, or with it.*
*And I know many pleasant things it will do to you.*

*"Wherefore Wildlife Ecology,"*
The River of the Mother of God and Other Essays

Leopold "wildlifer" Dan Thompson and his research partner were driving south on U.S. Highway 51 on Thursday, April 22, 1948. "When the news of Aldo Leopold's death came over the radio, we gasped and blankly looked at each other. I turned off the radio and we drove on for another thirty minutes in silence."[1] Dan's thoughts drifted back to the howl of a single wolf he had heard the evening before. He wondered "if the wolf had sensed the passing of a kindred spirit of the wilderness."[2]

Aldo Leopold turned the American Dream upside down. He was born in a mansion and died at a shack; yet the Shack was the home of his greatest riches. His book, "Great Possessions," was published after his death under the title, *A Sand County Almanac and Sketches Here and There.*[3-6] In it, Leopold invites his readers to sit with him at the Shack, to listen, to observe, and to think about the question: How can we live on the land without spoiling it?

The vivid urgency of this question has only heightened since Leopold's death. The popularity of his essays has proven this, and the prevailing

University of Wisconsin-Madison Archives X25 683

*The Gila Wilderness Area—the first region in the national forest system specifically set aside to be kept wild. As the person responsible for creating the designation, Leopold is called the "Father of the National Forest Wilderness System." The system now includes 548 wilderness areas in 44 states, and encompasses 95 million acres.*[7] *Because of the high use these areas receive, many people want to see more created. At the same time, there is pressure to release the existing areas for motorized recreation, lumbering, grazing, and mining—as the proponents of this plan say, for "wise use."*

clarity of his insights is written across the lands he loved. In June 1984, when the University of Wisconsin Arboretum and Wild Life Refuge held its fiftieth anniversary celebration, the face of the restored land bloomed healthy, fresh, and vibrant—a testament to the natural riches Wisconsin was meant to have.

The Shack's land, too, tells a story of tolerance, beauty, and respect. After Leopold's death, farmers in the area turned their "back forties" around the Shack property—a total of 1,200 acres—into a management trust.[8] As one travels over the curving drive to face the Shack, Aldo's landscaping comes to view. Sheltered in a cove of fifty-year-old pines, the beloved chicken coop peers over a prairie filled with swaying yellow coneflowers, liatris, big bluestem, and side-oats gama grass. Deer, grouse, woodcocks, bears, and other wildlife have found appealing habitat here. The land trust,

University of Wisconsin–Madison Arboretum (photo by Jean Lang–UIR Program)

*Curtis Prairie at the Wisconsin Arboretum, ca. 1990.*

called the Leopold Memorial Reserve, with the Bradley Study Center located there, serves as a land laboratory for selected research.

Even beyond the wilderness areas, the arboretum, and the Shack preserve, Leopold helped establish Wisconsin's Scientific Areas system, which consists of over 200 areas (more than 25,000 acres) set aside for land studies.[9] He guided the development of the precepts for these areas, and he fervently promoted the legislation that created the system, one of the most unique and successful of its kind in the United States.

Though Aldo never pressured them to do so, all his children became scientists and conservationists. Starker was a premier wildlife ecologist (he died in 1983). Luna is renowned for his pioneering work in river

Marybeth Lorbiecki

*The Shack today. Shack journal entry by JK, a family friend, for Saturday, June 19, 1965, reads: "It was Dorothy's first visit to the storied 'Shack.' As she looked across the prairie meadow and over the marshes to the vistas of hills and woods, she exclaimed at the happy fortune which had led the Leopolds to find 'such an* unmolested *corner of natural beauty!' It is hard not to feel that way now, even if one does know the facts. . . . Now the deer trails through the pines, the sweet fern on the sand-blows, the tamarack bogs, the meadows and openings are all blending together so naturally that it is hard to realize how much long-range forethought and what carefully integrated planning has been carried through here."*[10]

hydrology. After studying wildlife in various areas around the world, Nina and her second husband, Charles Bradley, are currently working on prairie restoration at the Shack property. Carl is a plant physiologist, researching seed viability and world agricultural problems. And Estella is a paleobotanist, tracking the continent's history of vegetation. Starker, Luna, and Estella have all been members of the National Academy of Sciences. No other family can boast this many members.

Leopold's children, students, and readers have kept the flame of his ethics and ecology burning—"Pluck a petal from a pasque flower, and you disturb a star."[11] Because of their efforts and others like them, we can still find places in America that feel natural, wild, and free. We may still hear a wolf call in the distance, watch a sord of mallards fly overhead, taste pine in the air, or find that pasque flower.

# A Daughter's Reflections[1]

## by Nina Leopold Bradley

*I had always wanted to own my own land,*
*and to study and enrich its fauna and flora by my own effort.*
*My wife, my three sons, and my two daughters,*
*each in his own individual manner,*
*have discovered deep satisfactions of one sort or another*
*in the husbandry of wild things on our own land.*

*Unpublished Foreword to* Great Possessions *manuscript*[2]

In an essay found amongst my father's works, he had written, "There are two things that interest me: the relation of people to each other, and the relation of people to land."

As a place to put such ideas to work, my father bought a "sand farm" in 1935 along the Wisconsin River, "first worn out and then abandoned by our bigger-and-better society."[3] This land had been "lived on" and been "destroyed" by its former owners. If you were selecting a piece of land to purchase, would this be what you would look for?

The sand farm was purchased for $8.00 an acre. Over the next thirteen years, our family, friends, and neighbors worked with "shovel and axe" to try to bring life back to the depleted acres of river bottom. The poor farm became a place where these two interests found voice—the relation of our family members to each other and their relation to this piece of land. It was a rich source of experience, a family retreat, and an outdoor laboratory.

Today I wonder if my father had any idea what a learning process this restoration was to become—not only for himself, but for his gang of kids.

Marybeth Lorbiecki

*View of the Wisconsin River from the Shack property.*

We discovered many things:

That a good way of learning about ecology is to try to restore an ecosystem. By attempting to bring back the native vegetation, we learned which plants get along together and which do not—and what a remarkable landscape architect nature is.

That "sun, wind, and rain," and the thrust of life would again and again determine the outcome of all our hard work.

That something more important than pines and prairie would come out of this experience and this Wisconsin soil. Family camaraderie grew and expanded—never to die.

Rarely has so small a place as this sand farm been studied and loved and looked after so long and so intimately. At the Shack, Father gradually clarified his understanding of ecological processes and land qualities—integrity, stability, and beauty—which he saw as the ingredients around which a land ethic could be built. Here, more than anywhere else, my father found the sense of place he had been seeking, and so have I. We all became participants in the drama of the land's interrelationships. As Father transformed the land, the land transformed him . . . and us.

*A sketch of some Shack essentials from Volume 4 of the Shack journals. June 12, 1965*
"Breakfast was gay, and we were relaxed and happy. What a place the dear old Shack is for making us all love the woods and each other!" E.B.L.

# NOTES

Many quotations have appeared in more than one source; thus, I will mention the source I used that provided the fullest quotation. For the most comprehensive life context for all quotations, Meine's biography, *Aldo Leopold: His Life and Work,* is the best source.

All references to *A Sand County Almanac* refer to the expanded edition: *A Sand County Almanac with Essays on Conservation from Round River* (New York: Ballantine Books, 1990).

## INTRODUCTION

1 "The State of the Profession," *The River of the Mother of God and Other Essays,* Ed. Susan L. Flader and J. Baird Callicott. (Madison: The University of Wisconsin Press, 1991) 280.

## LUG-INS-LAND

1 Charles Starker's son Arthur was a grain dealer, but he was rumored to have leanings toward design. Steven Brower, who researched the Starker family, says it may have been Arthur Starker's idea to model Burlington's Snake Alley (one of Charles Starker's—and the city's—triumphs) after narrow, curving passages he had observed in Europe. Arthur was sickly from birth; he died a bachelor in 1893.

2 The Starkers doted on their children and grandchildren. Charles and Marie had seven children, five of whom died after weaning, in their second summers. (Perhaps the deaths were due in part to food allergies, since the diagnosis was either "stomach complaint" or a problem with the bowels, and allergies did run in the family.)

3 Flader, Susan L. "Aldo Leopold: A Historical and Philosophical Perspective," speech to Des Moines County Historical Society, April 17, 1980; Starker-Leopold Collection.

4 Undated clipping from what is thought to be the *Burlington Hawkeye,* June 24, 1894, in the files of Steven R. Brower, Burlington, Iowa, quoted in "The Starker-Leopold Family Research Paper," draft, 1980; Starker-Leopold Collection.

5 *Biographical Review of Des Moines County, Iowa.* (Chicago: Hobart Publishing Company, 1905) 1070; Starker-Leopold Collection.

6 Meine, Curt. *Aldo Leopold: His Life and Work.* (Madison: University of Wisconsin Press, 1988) 14.

7 Every Saturday, Clara baked a cake for the Sunday picnic. Aldo had an insatiable sweet tooth and he more than once snitched the cake; so his mother locked it in a tin. Even this did not dissuade the young thief. He sawed off the lock. That's when his father stepped in, and Aldo withdrew from his life of crime.

8 Voegeli, Jim. "Remembering Aldo Leopold." Radio documentary on Aldo Leopold, c. 1974, tape; Starker-Leopold Collection.

9 Leopold, Frederic. "Leopold Family Anecdotes," transcripts from interview tapes with Elenor Lundgren; Starker-Leopold Collection.

10 Ibid.

11 Voegeli.

12 "What is a Weed?" *The River of the Mother of God,* 307

13 Leopold, Frederic. "A Hunter's Lesson." *Wild River Ramblings,* newsletter of the Des Moines County [Iowa] Conservation Board. 2, no. 3 (spring 1989); Starker-Leopold Collection.

14 "Good Oak," *A Sand County Almanac,* 16.

15 "Red Legs Kicking," ibid, 129.

16 Composition book; Aldo Leopold Papers, University of Wisconsin Archives.

17 Clipping from Feb. 10, 1900; Starker-Leopold Collection. The headlines read: "Charles Starker, Woven in the History of Burlington for Fifty Years; He Died Last Night; After Living Just a Half Century in This City, A Many-Sided Man, Who Came Into Intimate Contact with the Interests of Hundreds of Our Citizens of All Classes."

## Ornithologists and Explorations

1 Leopold, Frederic. "Aldo's School Years: Summer Vacation." April 1981; Starker-Leopold Collection. Published version in Thomas Tanner's *Aldo Leopold: The Man and His Legacy* (Ankeny, IA: Soil Conservation Society, 1987) 145.

2 Carl Leopold, Sr., became a great golf enthusiast, despite his son's chagrin about the game (which lasted his entire life.) In an article entitled, "How Carl Leopold Became a Convert to the Noble Game," in the *Burlington Hawkeye,* September 10, 1901, Carl is quoted "There is no game that fits so well the business and professional man, old or young. I once believed that duck and snipe shooting was the finest thing on earth, and for twenty-five years, I followed the gun and dog, and I have concluded lately that I will have to yield to golf." (Clara also thought the game excellent. In fact, she was the one who pushed Carl to try it for the sake of the children, so they would learn.) News clipping in the collection of Steven Brower of Burlington, Iowa.

3 Leopold, Frederic. "Aldo's School Years: Summer Vacation."

4 Ibid.

5 Gibbons, Boyd. "A Durable Scale of Values." *National Geographic (*November 1981) 685.
6 Leopold, Frederic. "Aldo's School Years: Summer Vacation."
7 Composition book; Aldo Leopold Papers.
8 Hunger, Edwin. Untitled, undated memoir; Starker-Leopold Collection.
9 Ibid.
10 Journal 1903; Aldo Leopold Papers.
11 Ibid.

## The Naturalist Out East

1 Hunger; Starker-Leopold Collection.
2 Fox, Stephen. *The American Conservation Movement: John Muir and His Legacy* (Madison: University of Wisconsin Press, 1981) 109.
3 Pinchot's application of basic principle of utilitarian philosophy; ibid, 111.
4 Gibbons, 685.
5 Letter; Aldo Leopold Papers.
6 Meine (1988) 35.
7 "The Maintenance of Forests," *The River of the Mother of God,* 39.
8 Ibid.
9 Meine (1988) 38.
10 Ibid, 44.
11 Ibid, 41.
12 Gibbons, 685.
13 Flader (1980).
14 Meine (1988) 44.
15 Ibid, 25.

## Women and Wise Use

1 Meine (1988) 55.
2 Ibid, 35.
3 Ibid, 55.
4 A year after he became friends with Bennie, Aldo wrote: "I feel I get quite as many new ideas from Benny [sic] as he does from me." Ibid, 66.
5 Ibid, 59.
6 Ibid, 67.
7 Ibid.
8 Ibid, 70.
9 Fox, 130.
10 First edition of the *Forest Service Field Manual,* Meine (1988) 77.
11 Meine (1988) 72.
12 Ibid, 74.

13 Ibid, 79.
14 Letter, Aldo Leopold Papers.
15 Ibid.
16 Letter, April 9, 1909; Aldo Leopold Papers.
17 Letter, Jan. 20, 1909; Aldo Leopold Papers.

## A Cowboy in Love

1 "The Busy Season," *The River of the Mother of God,* 40.
2 A. C. Ringland quoted; Voegeli.
3 These duties were outlined in the 1905 field manual: *The Use of the National Forest Reserves: Regulations and Instructions.* Meine (1988) 77.
4 Meine (1988) 90.
5 Letter, Oct. 7, 1909; Aldo Leopold Papers.
6 Flader (1980).
7 Letter, Oct. 4, 1909; Aldo Leopold Papers.
8 "Thinking Like a Mountain," *A Sand County Almanac,* 138.
9 Letter to his mother, Oct. 7, 1909; Aldo Leopold Papers.
10 Meine (1988) 99.
11 Ibid, 98.
12 Caption on photos in Aldo Leopold Papers, explanation in Meine (1988) 101.
13 Meine (1988) 100.
14 Ibid, 103.
15 Estella's full name was Maria Alvira Estella Bergere. She was born on August 24, 1890.
16 Meine (1988) 106.
17 Ibid, 107.
18 Ibid, 108.
19 Ibid, 109.
20 Ibid.
21 Letter, July 7, 1911; Aldo Leopold Papers. Within a few years, Jamie and Aldo became close friends and hunting partners.
22 Letter, May 23, 1911; Aldo Leopold Papers.
23 Meine (1988) 112.
24 Ibid, 113.
25 Letter to Estella, May 12, 1911; Aldo Leopold Papers.
26 Estella's mother was married and widowed before she married Alfred Bergere. Estella's family included two half-brothers and one half-sister in addition to—eventually—seven sisters and two brothers

## New Life and Near Death

1 "To the Forest Officers of the Carson," *The River of the Mother of God,* 43.
2 Meine (1988) 118.

3 Work journal; Aldo Leopold Papers.
4 Meine (1988) 120.
5 Gibbons, 690.
6 Meine (1988) 120.
7 Gibbons, 696.
8 Work journal; Aldo Leopold Papers.
9 Meine (1988) 123.
10 Ibid, 124.
11 Ibid.
12 Ibid, 125.
13 "To the Forest Officers of the Carson," *The River of the Mother of God*, 43-4.
14 Ibid, 43.
15 Ibid, 44.
16 Ibid, 46.
17 Meine (1988) 131.
18 Quotation book; Aldo Leopold Papers.
19 Ibid.
20 Meine (1988) 133.

## Save that Game

1 Acceptance speech for the Gold Medal from the Permanent Wild Life Protection Fund, Meine (1988) 161.
2 Meine (1988) 136-7.
3 Ibid, 136.
4 Ibid, 144-5.
5 The Grand Canyon became a national park on Feb. 26, 1919.
6 Meine (1988) 146.
7 Ibid, note #11, 549.
8 Ibid, 151.
9 Ibid, 150.
10 "The Varmint Question," *The River of the Mother of God*, 47.
11 Ibid.
12 Meine (1988) 152.
13 Ibid, 158.
14 Wild life (two words back then) was a relatively new term at the time. Eventually, a shift in attitude prompted people to start referring to game as wildlife.
15 Meine (1988) 161.
16 Letter; Aldo Leopold Papers.
17 Meine (1988) 161.
18 Ibid.
19 Ibid, 163.
20 Ibid, 167.
21 Ibid, 162.

22 August 1918 issue; Aldo Leopold Papers.

23 Address to Albuquerque Women's Club, Sept. 1918; Aldo Leopold Papers.

24 Ibid.

25 Meine (1988) 171.

26 Letter, April 22, 1919; Aldo Leopold Papers.

27 Meine (1988) 174.

28 Ibid, 173.

## A Wild Proposal

1 Meine (1988) 177.

2 "Some Fundamentals of Conservation in the Southwest," *The River of the Mother of God,* 96.

3 "Marshland Elegy," *A Sand County Almanac,* 108.

4 Meine (1988) 178.

5 Ibid, 179.

6 Ibid, 185.

7 Obituary of Charles Knesal Cooperrider, July 1948, *Journal of Wildlife Management*; republished in *Aldo Leopold's Wilderness* (Harrisburg, PA: Stackpole Books, 1990) 229.

8 Speech entitled "Erosin and Prosperity" as quoted in Meine (1988) 188. In a 1924 article for *Sunset Magazine* entitled "Pioneers and Gullies," (also in *The River of the Mother of God,* 107) Leopold wrote, "The loss of our existing farms we dismiss as an act of God—like a storm or the earthquake, inevitable. . . .On the contrary, it is the direct result of our own misuse of the country we are trying to improve."

9 Meine (1988) 187.

10 Carter, Luther J. "The Leopolds: A Family of Naturalists," *Science* (207, March 7, 1980) 1053.

11 Letter from Evan W. Kelley to Leopold, Nov. 13, 1944, describing past; Aldo Leopold Papers.

12 Meine (1988) 192.

13 Letter to Evan Kelley on occasion of Kelley's retirement, Oct. 13, 1944; Aldo Leopold Papers.

14 Assistant Forester Roy Headley wrote this about Leopold in Jan. 1922, Meine (1988) 197.

15 "The Wilderness and Its Place in Forest Recreational Policy," *The River of the Mother of God,* 79.

16 Ibid.

17 Ibid, 81.

18 Meine (1988) 201.

19 "The Green Lagoons," *A Sand County Almanac,* 151.

20 Ibid, 157.

21 *Watershed Handbook;* Aldo Leopold Foundation (Baraboo, WI).

22 "Some Fundamentals of Conservation in the Southwest," *The River of the Mother of God,* 92.

23 Meine (1988) 217.
24 Debate over burn policies still rages, as was demonstrated during the great Yellowstone fires of 1988.
25 "Some Fundamentals of Conservation in the Southwest," *The River of the Mother of God,* 94.
26 Ibid, 95.
27 "Conservation Esthetic," *A Sand County Almanac,* 295.
28 Letter; March 9, 1923; Aldo Leopold Papers
29 "Wilderness as a Form of Land Use," *The River of the Mother of God,* 135.
30 Meine (1988) 248.

## Surveying the Field

1 *Game Management,* as quoted by Clay Schoenfeld in "Fifty Years of Aldo Leopold's 'Game Management.'" *Wisconsin Academy Review* (September 1982) 3.
2 Meine (1988) 232.
3 Ibid, 68.
4 Ibid, 233.
5 Letter to Estella, July 5, 1924; Aldo Leopold Papers.
6 Ibid.
7 Ibid.
8 Meine (1988) 232.
9 Ibid, 79.
10 Ibid, 234.
11 Letter from Aldo in San Francisco, Aug. 7, 1927; Aldo Leopold Papers.
12 Ibid.
13 "Round River," *A Sand County Almanac,* 197.
14 Meine (1988) 182.
15 Ibid.
16 "A Man's Leisure Time," *A Sand County Almanac,* 181.
17 *Daily News* clipping, 1934; Aldo Leopold Papers.
18 "A Man's Leisure Time," *A Sand County Almanac,* 186-7.
19 Author interview with Nina Leopold Bradley, July 1991. Though generally calm and soft-spoken, Aldo occasionally reached a boiling point. Once, while he was clamping feathers on a set of arrows and Carl and Nina were roughhousing around him, he locked them in a closet for a little while to calm them down. (Tanner, 169) In contrast, a few years after the closet incident, Starker loaned the family's new blue Chevy sedan to his girlfriend Aggie for a short ride. She had an accident and totaled the car. Aldo's response was to ask if Aggie was hurt. When he found out she was fine, he turned to Estella and said, "Please ask Aggie to dinner so she will not think we are angry with her for wrecking the car." (Luna Leopold, Foreword to *Aldo Leopold: The Professor*, viii.)
20 Carter, 1052.

21 Letter to Kermit Roosevelt, Secretary of the Boone and Crockett Club, April 22, 1927; Aldo Leopold Papers.

22 Letter to Estella from Iowa City, Aug. 7, 1928; ibid.

23 Untitled, undated paper of Vivian Horn's memories; Aldo Leopold Papers. For published version, see McCabe, Robert. *Aldo Leopold: The Professor* (Amherst, WI: Palmer Publications, 1987) 18.

24 Ibid.

25 Letter to Estella from Iowa City, Aug. 7, 1928; Aldo Leopold Papers.

26 Meine (1988) 264.

27 1947 draft of foreword for Leopold's proposed book "Great Possessions," which became *A Sand County Almanac.* This draft, rejected by Leopold, was published in the appendix to *Companion to a Sand County Almanac,* J. Baird Callicott ed. (Madison; University of Wisconsin) 284.

28 Undated news clipping from *American Game*; Aldo Leopold Papers.

29 News clipping, Dec. 15, 1930, ibid.

30 Ibid.

31 McCabe, Robert A., 103.

32 News clipping, Sept. 1933; Aldo Leopold Papers.

33 Meine (1988) 279.

34 Ibid. Leopold has been called the "Father of Wildlife Management" (McCabe, Robert 89). His book *Game Management* is still in print and in use.

35 "Game and Wild Life Conservation," *The River of the Mother of God,* 165.

36 Ibid.

37 Meine (1988) 174.

38 "Helping Ourselves," *The River of the Mother of God,* 205.

39 Explanation of the origination of these terms from *Thinking Like a Mountain,* Susan L. Flader (Columbia: University of Missouri Press, 1977) 5.

40 *Game Management,* reprinted (Madison: University of Wisconsin Press, 1986) dedication page.

41 Ibid, vii.

42 Ibid, 423.

43 Meine (1988) 301.

44 Ibid, 312.

45 "Ecology and Politics," *The River of the Mother of God,* 286.

46 "Illinois Bus Ride," *A Sand County Almanac,* 126.

47 "Conservation Economics," *The River of the Mother of God,* 197.

48 "Conservation Ethic," ibid, 183.

49 Ibid, 191.

50 Ibid.

51 Gilbert, Bil. "Sand County' Farm Shaped New Ethic Environment" *Smithsonian* (Oct. 1980) 137.

## The Land Laboratories

1 News clipping, 1934; Aldo Leopold Papers.

2 Meine (1988) 307.
3 Untitled, undated paper of Vivian Horn's memories; Aldo Leopold Papers.
4 Butcher, Clifford F. "Every Farm in Wisconsin To Be a Game Preserve," *Milwaukee Journal*, Sunday, Jan. 5, 1936. news clipping; Aldo Leopold Papers.
5 Meine (1988) 310.
6 Meine, Curt. "The Farmer as Conservationist." in Tanner, 46.
7 Aldo helped Luna set up an unprecedented college program with courses in "botany, ecology, soils, geology, and engineering to prepare for work in the unknown field of soil conservation." Luna was partway through his coursework when the Soil Erosion Service was established. (Letter from Luna Leopold to Walter C. Gumbel, April 22, 1948; Aldo Leopold Papers.)
8 "Coon Valley: An Adventure in Cooperative Conservation," *The River of the Mother of God*, 218.
9 H. Albert Hochbaum quoted. McCabe, Richard. *Aldo Leopold: Mentor* (Madison: Department of Wildlife Ecology, University of Wisconsin, 1988) 54.
10 Meine (1988) 317.
11 McCabe, Richard, 51.
12 Meine (1988) 324.
13 Ibid.
14 "The Arboretum and the University," *The River of the Mother of God*, 211.
15 Ibid, 210. Because of later funding problems, only a fraction of Leopold's wildlife plan for the university arboretum was actually carried out. Yet the parts that were implemented were innovative and successful.
16 Meine (1988) 329.
17 Letter, "Invitation to Help Organize a Group to Preserve the American Wilderness," Oct. 19, 1934; Aldo Leopold Papers.
18 Meine (1988) 248.
19 Ibid, 343. During this time, Leopold was a member of so many professional groups and maintained such a pace of work activity that he didn't always know what was "in." Starker remembered when his father asked him who the Green Bay Packers were.
20 First Shack journal; Aldo Leopold Papers.
21 Ibid.
22 Meine (1988) 359. On December 20, 1935, Leopold wrote a letter to Editor Herbert Smith of the *Journal of Forestry* in response to the editorial "The Cult of the Wilderness." Leopold said: "To fully appreciate what it means to live in a country which has plenty of forests and wild life, but which has lost all its wildness, one must go to Germany and see the annual exodus of hunters and hikers to the still partly-wild Carpathians." Aldo Leopold Papers.
23 "The Last Stand," *The River of the Mother of God*, 292.
24 Ibid, 293.
25 Meine (1988) 356.
26 Butcher (news clipping).

27 Ibid.

28 "Engineering and Conservation," *The River of the Mother of God,* 254.

29 Meine (1988) 353.

30 Ibid, 358.

31 Ibid, 357.

32 "Reflections and Recollections," Tanner, 170.

33 Foreword, *A Sand County Almanac,* xviii.

34 Ibid.

35 Like Aldo's mother Clara, Estella was quite musical, and she passed this talent on to her children. Aldo could whistle, but he was so shy that he rarely did so; he never sang.

36 "Song of the Gavilan," *A Sand County Almanac,* 158.

37 1947 rejected foreword to ms "Great Possessions" *Companion to A Sand County Almanac,* 286.

38 "Planning for Wildlife," a Sept. 26, 1941, unpublished essay referred to by Curt Meine in "The Utility of Preservation and the Preservation of Utility," in *The Wilderness Condition,* (San Francisco, CA: Sierra Club Books) 156.

39 "Round River," *A Sand County Almanac,* 190.

40 Draft of essay published in *Living Wilderness,* Vol. 1, Sept. 1935; Aldo Leopold Papers.

## The Professor

1 Marie McCabe, the wife of graduate student Robert McCabe, was quite surprised when she first met the Professor. "I had expected him to be a combination of Abe Lincoln and Thomas Jefferson. Here he was, extremely gracious, but of ordinary size and appearance, not at all handsome . . . showing no sign of being an author and absolute authority on everything." (McCabe, Robert, 4.) Robert S. Ellarson, a Leopold wildlifer, recalled his first meeting: "The class had assembled before the Professor arrived. Soon the clicking of steel-cleated heels signalled his approach. When he arrived and stood before the class, I was impressed by the bold, virile, almost macho appearance of the man. And I was absolutely enthralled by the lecture that followed." McCabe, Richard E., 13.

2 "Natural History," *A Sand County Almanac,* 208.

3 McCabe, Robert, 60.

4 H. Albert Hochbaum quoted. McCabe, Richard, 56.

5 "Wildlife in American Culture," quoted by Paul Errington in his obituary "In Appreciation of Aldo Leopold," *Journal of Wildlife Management,* (12, no. 4, October 1948); Aldo Leopold Papers.

6 From Leopold's teaching notes, McCabe, Robert, 161.

7 "Wherefore Wildlife Education," *The River of the Mother of God,* 336.

8 One example of this type of reference for themselves by his students is by Frances Hamerstrom: McCabe, Richard, 3.

9 James B. Hall quoted. Ibid, 26.

10 Arthur S. Hawkins quoted. Ibid, 40.
11 Frances Hamerstrom quoted. Ibid, 30-1.
12 Ernie Swift, a supporter of Leopold's in the Wisconsin Conservation Department throughout the deer debates, said of Aldo, "You would go out with him, and he'd stretch your brains until they were tired." Meine (1988) 397.
13 Daniel Thompson quoted. McCabe, Richard, 104.
14 Frederick Hamerstrom quoted. Ibid, 34.
15 Lyle K. Sowls quoted. Ibid, 82-3.
16 Frederick Hamerstrom quoted. Ibid, 34.
17 H. Albert Hochbaum quoted. Ibid, 63.
18 Ibid.
19 McCabe, Robert, 15.
20 Meine (1988) 378.
21 McCabe, Richard, 25.
22 Untitled, undated paper of Vivian Horn's memories; Aldo Leopold Papers.
23 Ibid.
24 Meine (1988) 392.
25 "Sky Dance," *A Sand County Almanac,* 33.
26 Nina Leopold Bradley, author interview.
27 Meine (1988) 396.

## Paths of Violence

1 Meine (1988) 393.
2 Ibid, 456.
3 Bruce P. Stollberg quoted: McCabe, Robert, 55.
4 Gilbert, 138.
5 From "Phenological Record for Sauk and Dane Counties, Wisconsin, 1935-1945," published in *Ecological Monographs,* referred to in unpublished speech "Personal Reflections of a Daughter," by Nina Leopold Bradley in 1991 at annual meeting of Soil and Water Conservation Society.
6 Richard D. Taber quoted: McCabe, Richard, 100.
7 "Conservation Blueprints," published in *American Forests*, Dec. 1937, as referred to in Meine (1988) 402.
8 Letter to Leopold, July 7, 1943; Aldo Leopold Papers.
9 Meine (1988) 447.
10 Ibid, 444.
11 "Adventures of a Conservation Commissioner," *The River of the Mother of God,* 331.
12 Meine (1988) 452.
13 Ibid, 468.
14 Carter, 1053.
15 Meine (1988) 469.
16 Ibid.

17 Ibid, 457.
18 Ibid.
19 Ibid, 453.
20 Ibid, 454.
21 Gibbons, 684.
22 Meine (1988) 455.
23 Ibid, 456.
24 "Thinking Like a Mountain," *A Sand County Almanac,* 138.
25 Ibid.
26 "Round River," ibid, 189-90.
27 Meine (1988) 467.
28 Ibid, 473.

## Great Possessions

1 Meine (1988) 477.
2 "Axe in Hand," *A Sand County Almanac,* 74.
3 "The Ecologocial Conscience," ibid, 246.
4 "The State of the Profession," *The River of the Mother of God,* 280.
5 "The Ecological Conscience," ibid, 340.
6 Ibid, 345.
7 "The Outlook," *A Sand County Almanac,* 263.
8 Ibid.
9 "The Ethical Sequence," ibid, 239.
10 "Wherefore Wildlife Ecology," *The River of the Mother of God,* 337.
11 "The Role of Wildlife in a Liberal Education," ibid, 303.
12 Meine (1988) 506.
13 Ibid.
14 "January Thaw," *A Sand County Almanac,* 3.
15 Meine (1988) 509.
16 Ibid, 510.
17 Ibid.
18 Ibid, 517.
19 McCabe, Robert, 142.

## Afterword

1 McCabe, Richard, 108.
2 Ibid.
3 At the time of his death, Aldo had several projects in view for the future. He planned to revise *Game Management*, which he saw as "sadly out of date" (Meine (1988) 523). And he hoped to return someday to the case histories he had collected for "Southwestern Game Fields" to examine them from an ecological perspective. He planned to work as a full-time professor until his retirement, and then build a year-

round home on the Shack property.

4 Aldo was buried in the cemetery his Grandfather Starker designed—Aspen Grove Cemetery in Burlington. The two brothers married to two sisters—Aldo and Estella, Carl and Dolores—now lie next to the Starker mausoleum. Estella Bergere Leopold died in 1975. Two large white oaks and two white pines shade the simple stones.

5 Within days of Aldo's death, Luna and his wife Carolyn, Carl and his wife Keena, and Nina and her husband Bill all welcomed babies into their families (the latter two were firstborns). Estella, Sr., was overcome by grief at Aldo's death, but the grandchildren kept her busy and helped her heal. It took many years, however, before she began to make a new life for herself.

6 Clara Leopold, who had remained close to her eldest son all her life, died within a month of Aldo, at the age of eighty-eight.

7 Statistics on present wilderness areas were taken from a fact sheet compiled by Forester Christine Ryan in 1993. Though Leopold has been called the "Father of the National Forest Wilderness System," some people argue that Arthur Carhart should be given the title since records suggest that he submitted the first proposal to set aside a federal forest area as wilderness (in the Superior National Forest in 1922). Others argue that Leopold talked about the wilderness preservation idea as early as 1913, and that he prepared a specific proposal for the Gila region a year before Carhart made his first proposal. Leopold's proposal was unquestionably the first to succeed in creating a designated wilderness area. The two men supported each other's plans and would probably find the entire discussion ridiculous.

8 In 1978, the Shack was listed on the National Register of Historic Places. It has been called "the most famous chicken coop in the world."

9 McCabe, Richard, 71.

10 Shack journal; Aldo Leopold Papers.

11 "Built on Honor to Endure," speech by Sharon Kaufman, Sept. 16, 1986; Starker-Leopold Collection.

## A Daughter's Reflections

1 "Personal Reflection of a Daughter." Essay based on a speech given at the 1991 annual meeting of the Soil and Water Conservation Society.

2 Unpublished foreword to "Great Possessions" manuscript, *A Companion to A Sand County Almanac*, 287.

3 Foreword, *A Sand County Almanac*, xviii.

# Works by Aldo Leopold

*Aldo Leopold's Wilderness: Selected Early Writings by the Author of A Sand County Almanac.* David E. Brown and Neil B. Carmony, eds. Harrisburg, PA: Stackpole Books, 1990.

*Game Management.* Reprinted. Madison: The University of Wisconsin Press, 1986.

*Report on a Game Survey of the North Central States.* Madison: Democrat Printing Company for the Sporting Arms and Ammunitions Manufacturers' Institute, 1931.

*The River of the Mother of God and Other Essays.* Susan L. Flader and J. Baird Callicott, eds. Madison: University of Wisconsin Press, 1991.

*Round River.* Luna B. Leopöld, ed. New York: Oxford University Press, 1953.

*A Sand County Almanac.* New York: Oxford University Press, 1949.

*A Sand County Almanac with Essays on Conservation from Round River.* New York: Oxford University Press, 1996; New York: Ballantine, 1990.

*USFS Game and Fish Handbook.* USDA, USFS, D-3, December 1915.

*Watershed Handbook.* USFS, USDA, D-3, December 1923.

# Selected References

*→ suggested further reading*

Aldo Leopold Papers (Aldo's childhood letters, drawings, and ornithological journals, work journals, letters, quotation journals, archery journals, Shack journals, newspaper clippings, obituaries, reminiscences). Madison: University of Wisconsin Archives.

→*Aldo Leopold: A Prophet for All Seasons*. Video cassette, Metabasis. Minocqua, Wisconsin: Northword Press.

Bradley, Charles C. "Doctor of the Land, A Matter of Degree." *Wisconsin Academy Review* 34, no. 1 (December 1987) 7-23. (Author and his family were friends of the Leopolds in Madison.)

———. "A Short Story of a Man Hunt." *Wisconsin Academy Review* 26, no. 1 (December 1979) 7-9.

Bradley, Nina Leopold (daughter). Interview with author, Bradley home on Shack property, July 1991.

———. "Great Possessions." *Wisconsin Academy Review* 26, no. 1 (December 1979) 3.

———. "Personal Reflections of a Daughter." Speech given at the 1991 annual meeting of the Soil and Water Conservation Society.

Brower, Steven R. "The Starker-Leopold Family Research Paper." Draft. April 1980, Starker-Leopold Collection.

Callicott, J. Baird. *Companion to A Sand County Almanac: Interpretive and Critical Essays*. Madison: University of Wisconsin Press, 1987.

→Carter, Luther J. "The Leopolds: A Family of Naturalists." *Science* 207, March 7, 1980.

Flader, Susan L. "Aldo Leopold: A Historical and Philosophical Perspective." Speech to the Des Moines County Historical Society, April 17, 1980.

→Flader, Susan L. *Thinking Like a Mountain: Aldo Leopold and the Evolution of an Ecological Attitude Toward Deer, Wolves, and Forests.* Columbia, Missouri: University of Missouri Press, 1977.

Fox, Stephen. *The American Conservation Movement: John Muir and His Legacy.* Madison: University of Wisconsin Press, 1981.

→Gibbons, Boyd. "A Durable Scale of Values." *National Geographic*, November 1981.

→Gilbert, Bil. "'Sand Country' Farm Shaped a New Ethic for the Environment." *Smithsonian*, October 1980.

Hawkins, A.S. (first ed.), *Flyways: Pioneering Waterfowl Management in North America.* Washington: USDI, Fish and Wildlife Service, 1984.

Kaufman, Sharon. "Built on Honor to Endure." Speech given to Des Moines County Historical Society, September 16, 1986.

Leopold, Frederic (brother). Transcript of taped interview with Elenor Lundren, Starker-Leopold Collection.

———. "A Hunter's Lesson." *Wild River Ramblings: A Newsletter of the Des Moines County Conservation Board* 2, no. 3 (Spring 1989), Starker-Leopold Collection.

———. "Recollections of an Old Member [of Crystal Lake Hunt Club]." Speech given at club, March 1977, Starker-Leopold Collection.

→McCabe, Richard E., Ed. *Aldo Leopold: Mentor, by His Graduate Students.* Madison: Department of Wildlife Ecology, University of Wisconsin, 1988.

→McCabe, Robert A. *Aldo Leopold: The Professor (Reminiscences of an Assistant and Student).* Amherst, Wisconsin: Palmer Publications, 1987.

→Meine, Curt. *Aldo Leopold: His Life and Work.* Madison: University of Wisconsin Press, 1988. (This biography is in-depth, complete, and fascinating. It lists the most comprehensive life context for all quotations. As Gaylord Nelson says, "It's good fun to boot.")

———. "The Utility of Preservation and the Preservation of Utility: Leopold's Fine Line." In *The Wilderness Condition; Essays on Environment and Civilization*, ed. Max Oelschlaeger, San Francisco, CA: Sierra Club Books, 1992.

Norton, Bryan G. *Toward Unity Among Environmentalists.* New York: Oxford University Press, 1991.

✦Schoenfeld, Clay. "Aldo Leopold Remembered." *Audobon*, March-April 1978. (Author was one of Aldo's students.)

———. "Fifty years of Aldo Leopold's Game Management" and "An Aldo Leopold Album." *Wisconsin Academy Review* 28, no. 4 (Sept. 1982) 5-7.

Starker-Leopold Collection (news clippings, books, tapes, clothes, objects, speeches, papers, memoirs, and photos illuminating the prominent Burlington family). Burlington, Iowa: Des Moines County Historical Society.

✦Tanner, Thomas. *Aldo Leopold: The Man and His Legacy.* Ankeny, Iowa: Soil Conservation Society of America, 1987.

Voegeli, Jim. "Remembering Aldo Leopold." Radio documentary on Aldo Leopold through the eyes of the people who knew him best. (The entire collection of taped interviews—done from 1973-1974—is stored in the State Historical Society of Wisconsin Archives.)

✦*Wild by Law: Aldo Leopold, Bob Marshall, Howard Zahniser and the Redefinition of American Progress.* Film documentary by Lawrence Hott and Diane Garey, Florentine Films, 1991.

Zimmerman, James H. "Impressions of Aldo Leopold: A Student's View." *EE NEWS* 3, no. 3 (February 1987). Madison: Wisconsin Department of Natural Resources.

# INDEX


## A

Agriculture, conservation and 124–126, 136
Albuquerque Game Protective Association 74, 95
Albuquerque, New Mexico 39, 47, 62, 68, 72, 77–79
  Chamber of Commerce 77–79
Alfred A. Knopf, Inc. 168, 176, 177
Allison, J. Howard 45
American Association for the Advancement of Science 120–121
American Forestry Association 171
American Game Conference (1920) 86
American Game Conference (1928) 108
American Game Protective Association (AGPA) 71, 74, 81, 105, 109, 110, 111-113, 137. *See also* American Wildlife Institute
American Wildlife Institute 137
*Animal Ecology* (Elton) 116
Antonito, Colorado 47
Apache Nation 40
Apache National Forest 40, 41–45,, 87, 89, 167
Archery. *See* Hunting
*Arizona* (magazine) 74
Aspen Grove Cemetery 201
Avery, Carlos 110

## B

Baraboo, Wisconsin 133, 178
Barker, Elliot 77
Beck Committee 127–128
Beck, Thomas 127–128
Bergere, Alfred M. 50, 79, 192
Bergere, Eloisa Luna Otero 50, 63, 192
Bergere, Estella. *See* Leopold, Estella Bergere
Bergere, Luna 50, 54
Biodiversity 68
"Biotic View of Land, A" (Leopold) 161
Birds 14, 18–20, 29, 68
  Refuges 72, 86
Blue Mountains 42
Blue River 87
Boone and Crockett Club 12
Boundary Waters Canoe Area 90, 97, 102. *See also* Wilderness
Bradley, Charles 184
Bradley, Nina Leopold. *See* Leopold, Nina
Bradley Study Center 183
Bright's disease (Nephritis) 57–58, 74
Broome, Harvey 132
Brower, Steven 189
Bryant and Stratton Business College 5
*Burlington Democrat-Journal* 14
*Burlington Hawkeye* 4, 190
Burlington High School 17–18
Burlington, Iowa 1–3, 5, 29, 58, 61, 97, 189, 201
Buss, Irv 148

## C

*Canvasback on a Prairie Marsh* (Hochbaum) 164
Carhart, Arthur 84, 85, 86, 90, 94, 97, 201
Carl Schurz Memorial Foundation 134
Carpathian Mountains 197
Carson National Forest 47, 51, 53–54, 56, 83
*Carson Pine Cone* 39, 49, 58, 61. See also *Pine Cone*
*Century* (magazine) 24
Chapman, Frank M. 18

Charles Scribner's Sons, Inc. 116
Chicago Field Museum 130
Chiricahua National Forest 47
Civil service exams 37
Civilian Conservation Corps (CCC) 120, 126, 131
Cleveland, Grover 22, 24
*Collier's Weekly* (magazine) 127
*Condor, The* (magazine) 113
Conservation 26–27, 124, 145, 161
  Ethics 174–175
"Conservation Esthetic, A" (Leopold) 161
"Conservation Ethic, The" (Leopold speech) 121
Conservation movement 22-24, 35, 42, 59, 71, 75, 109, 110, 112, 114, 121–122, 137, 142–143, 156, 158, 160–161, 174–175
*Conservation of Natural Resources, The* (Van Hise) 100
Coon Valley Conservation Project 126
Cooperrider, Charles 88
Crapo Park 3
Crystal Lake Hunt Club 10
Curtis, John 131, 167
Curtis Prairie 131

## D

Dane County, Wisconsin 115
Darling, Jay "Ding" 127–128, 137, 156
Darwin, Charles 31
Datil National Forest 83
Deer management 110–111, 161–164, 168, 174
"Deer Management in the Southwest" (Leopold) 110
Delta Duck Station, Manitoba, Canada 164
Doucette, Texas 37
Drummond, "Ham" 27
Dust Bowl 119–120, 132, 133–134, 145

## E

"Ecological Conscience, The" (Leopold) 174
Ecological Society of America 142, 171
Ecology 7–10, 13–14, 27–29, 102, 116, 142, 146–149, 153
"Economics, Philosophy, and Land" (Leopold) 161
Ecosystems 160
Elder, Bill 159, 201
Ellarson, Robert S. 198
Elton, Charles 116
Ely, Minnesota 97
Erosion. *See* Soil conservation
Errington, Paul 111, 164–165
Estes Park, Colorado 20

## F

Fassett, Norman 131
Faville Grove Wildlife Experimental Area 125–126
Faville, Stoughton 124–125
Fire management 93–94, 167–168, 195
*Ford Radio Hour* 156
Forest Products Laboratory 88, 95, 100, 105, 106
Forest Service 37, 39–40, 41, 42, 58, 61, 62–63, 65–66, 67–68, 71, 72, 73–74, 77, 81, 83–84, 87–96, 111, 160. *See also* individual national forests
  Origin of 24
  Wilderness and 84–86, 90–91
Forester's Club 33
Forestry xii, 21–24, 34–35, 58, 87, 105
  in Germany 134–135
  National Forests 22–24
*Forward Albuquerque* 77
Frank, Bernard 132
Franklin, Benjamin 61

## G

*Game and Fish Handbook* (Leopold) 68–71
Game cropping 125–126, 126
Game farms 109
Game management 12, 42, 61, 63, 65–66, 71–72, 73–74, 86, 107, 108, 109–114, 15–116, 129, 145, 153, 161–164
  in Germany 134
*Game Management* (Leopold) xi–xii, 97, 111, 114–115, 116–119, 200
"Game Policy in a Nutshell" (Leopold) 112
Game surveys 107–108, 109, 110
Germany 134–136, 197
Get-Away Club 102
Gila National Forest 90–91, 93, 96
Gila River 83
Gila Wilderness Area 90, 94, 96, 201
Good Roads Movement 94
Grand Canyon 68, 69, 74, 110, 193
Grange, Wallace 161
Graves, Henry 73, 81, 86
Grazing 35, 47, 49, 53–54, 62, 66, 77, 87, 88, 91, 93
Great Depression 119
Greeley, William B. 88–89, 95
Green Bay Packers 197
Grinnell, George Bird 12
Guthrie, John D. 41, 42

## H


Haeckel, Ernst 116
Hale, James B. 153
Hall, Harry C. 47–49, 51, 52, 54
Hamerstrom, Frances 148, 149
Hamerstrom, Frederick 148, 152
*Handbook of Birds of Eastern North America* (Chapman) 18
Harrison, Benjamin 22
Hawkins, Art 147
Headley, Roy 194
Hochbaum, Hans Albert 148, 164, 165–167, 168, 178
Hoover, Herbert 112–113
Horn, Vivian 107, 151, 152, 153, 158
Hornaday Plan 73
Hornaday, William T. 59, 71–72, 74, 109, 113, 119, 123
Hunger, Edwin 18–20, 22
*Hunter-Trader-Trapper* (magazine) 113
Hunting 10–12, 13, 15, 27, 33, 61, 76, 103–105, 108, 109, 110, 114, 133, 141, 166, 190
  Game management and 163
  in Germany 135–136
*Hunting with the Bow and Arrow* (Pope) 103


## I


Izaak Walton League 102, 105


## J


Jacobsky, Benjamin 32, 191
Jamison, H.B. "Jamie" 49, 51, 52, 192
Jicarilla Apache Reservation 56, 72
Jicarilla Mountains 56
Jiminy Hicks (horse) 40–41
Johnson, Robert Underwood 24
Johnston, Don P. 68
Jones, Sara Elizabeth (Libbie) 160
*Journal of Forestry* 90, 197


## K


Kaibab Plateau 110
Kelley, Major Evan 89, 95, 194
Kerr, John 66
Kisow, Sam 125
Kneipp, Leon 66, 71
Knights of Columbus 79
Kumlien Club 102


## L


Lake Huron 15
Lake Wingra 103, 130
"Land Ethic, The" 174
Land health 141–142
"Land Use and Democracy" (Leopold) 161
Lawrenceville School 24–26, 27
Lee, Orville 147
Leopold, Bruce Carl 173
Leopold, Carl (brother) 7, 81, 91, 97, 201
Leopold, Carl (father) 4, 5–7, 8–9, 11, 12–13, 16, 17, 21–22, 24, 33, 53, 58, 61, 63, 190
Leopold, Carl (son) 86, 114, 141, 158, 168–169, 184, 195, 201
Leopold, Carolyn Clugston 173, 201
Leopold, Charles (grandfather) 4–5
Leopold, Clara Starker (mother) 3, 4, 5–7, 10, 15, 24, 26, 35, 58, 97, 98, 190, 198, 201
Leopold Desk Company 16, 17, 111, 119
Leopold, Dolores Bergere 91, 201
Leopold, Estella (daughter) 105, 107, 114, 134, 141, 159, 173, 178–179, 184
Leopold, Estella Bergere (wife) 47, 49–50, 51–52, 53, 54, 58, 61, 62, 63, 66, 73, 81, 86, 89, 103, 107, 111, 118, 133, 134, 141, 152, 159, 169, 173, 175, 177, 178, 179, 192, 198, 201
Leopold, Frederic (brother) 7, 8, 29, 54, 79, 97
Leopold, Keena Rogers 158, 168, 201
Leopold, Luna (son) 72, 89, 97, 105, 114, 126, 127, 133, 141, 158, 173, 177–178, 183, 184, 197, 201
Leopold, Marie (sister) 7, 9, 32, 97
Leopold, Nina (daughter) 77, 104, 114, 137, 141, 154, 156, 184, 185–186, 195, 201
Leopold, Starker (son) 59, 61, 62, 66, 73, 74, 89, 97, 114, 126, 133, 141, 158, 183, 184, 195, 197
Leopold, Thusneld Runge (grandmother) 4–5
Leopold Memorial Reserve 182–183
Les Cheneaux Club 15, 29
Liberty, Missouri 4, 5
Lignon, J. Stokley 93
Lincoln, Abraham 98
*Living Wilderness, The* (journal) 142
London, Jack 10
Lone Tree Hunt Club 10
Longenecker, G. William 131

Lovejoy, P. S. 110, 113
Lug-ins-land 4

## M

MacKaye, Benton 132
Macmillan Publishing Co., Inc. 168
MacQuarrie, Gordon 162
Madison, Wisconsin 88, 95, 98–99, 107, 110
Magdalena, New Mexico 72
*Manual of Botany* (Gray) 27
Marquette Island, Michigan 15–16
Marsh, Ray 56
Marshall, Robert 95, 132
Matamek Conference 116
Mayo Clinic 176, 178
McCabe, Marie 198
McCabe, Robert 165, 171, 177, 178, 198
Miller, Gretchen 32
*Milwaukee Journal* 124, 162
Mogollon Mountains 90
Moore, Ellwood 147
More Game Birds for America Foundation 109
Mountain lions. *See* Predator control
Muir, John 22–24

## N

National Academy of Sciences 184
National Forests. *See* Forest Service; Forestry; Individual forests
National Parks 84
National Wilderness System 182, 201
National Wildlife Refuge System 73, 127–129
*Naturalist's Voyage Around the World, A* (Darwin) 31
New Mexico Game and Fish Commission 86
New Mexico Game Protective Association (NMGPA) 73, 74–76, 86–87
*New York Times* 123
North American Wildlife Conference (1936) 137

## O

Oberholzer, Ernest 95
Orr, George 27
*Our Vanishing Wild Life* (Hornaday) 58–59
Ouspensky, Piotr D. 94
*Outdoor Life* (magazine) 116
*Outdoor Pastimes of an American Hunter* (Roosevelt) 31
*Outings* (magazine) 10
Oxford University Press 178

## P

Page, "Poittie" 27
Pearl Harbor 158
Permanent Wild Life Protection Fund 75–76
Pettit, R. Fred 93, 110
Phenology 160
Photos/Illustrations
- Abercrombie, Mable 132
- Bakkom, Clifford 177
- Beer, James R. 177
- Bergere family 52
- Broome, Harvey 132
- Burlington, Iowa 2
- Carhart, Arthur 85
- Carson house 55
- Classroom materials 128, 129, 148, 169, 176
- Crystal Lake Hunt Club 11
- Curtis Prairie 183
- Darling, Jay "Ding" 127
- Delta Duck Station 165
- Department of Wildlife Management 151
- Drawings 14, 59
- Dust Bowl 119
- Emlin, Ginny and John 103
- Faville Grove Wildlife Experimental Area 125
- *Forward Albuquerque* 78
- Garden plans 67
- Gila Wilderness Area 182
- Grand Canyon 69
- Grazing effects 87
- Hale, James 168
- Hochbaum, Hans Albert 165
- Hornaday, William Temple 70
- Hunting journal 92, 166
- Jackson, Pepper 168
- Jamison, Jamie 50
- Jones, Sara Elizabeth "Libbie" 168
- Journal of Carl Leopold 140
- Lawrenceville School 25
- Leopold, Aldo 6, 9, 10, 16, 28, 33, 36, 37, 40, 44, 48, 50, 51, 55, 60, 99, 101, 103, 104, 138, 146, 147, 159, 165, 166, 168, 172, 173, 177
- Leopold, Bruce Carl 173
- Leopold, Carl (brother) 9
- Leopold, Carl (father) 8
- Leopold, Carl (son) 158
- Leopold, Clara Starker (mother) 98
- Leopold, Clara Starker and children 17
- Leopold Desks Insignia 16
- Leopold, Estella (daughter) 104, 118
- Leopold, Estella Bergere (wife) 46, 50,

51, 55, 60, 76, 103, 118, 138
Leopold family 80, 154, 155
Leopold, Frederic (brother) 55
Leopold, Luna (son) 118
Leopold, Marie (sister) 9
Leopold, Nina (daughter) 138
Leopold, Starker (son) 60, 76, 103, 139
Les Cheneaux 16
Logs on Mississippi River 22
Lug-ins-land 4
MacKaye, Benton 132
Madison house 100
Market hunter 13
Marsh, Ray 57
Marshall, Bob 132
McCabe, Robert 166
Muir, John 23
Pinchot, Gifford 23
Quotation notebook 62
Richards, Steven 177
Riley Game Cooperative 115
Ringland, Arthur 45
Roosevelt, Theodore 23
Sargent, Charles Sprague 23
"Shack, the" 133, 146, 154, 155, 159, 172, 177, 184, 186, 187
Spud (dog) 16
Starker, Charles 3
Starker, Marie Runge 3
Starr's Cave 20
Stoddard, Herbert 108
Survey crew 44
Thompson, Donald R. 177
Trappers Lake 84
University of Wisconsin—Arboretum 131, 168
Wisconsin farm 106
Wisconsin River 186
Wright, Bruce S. 177
Yale Forest School Camp 34
Pinchot, Gifford 24, 34–35, 73, 86
*Pine Cone* 72, 74, 79, 86. See also *Carson Pine Cone*
Pooler, Frank 86, 88, 91, 96
Pope, Saxton 103
Predator control 42, 43, 65, 72–73, 87, 109, 110–111, 142, 161, 163, 167–168
Prospect Hill Elementary School 9–10

## Q

Quetico Lake District. *See* Boundary Waters Canoe Area

## R

Rand, C. W. 5, 16
Rand, E. W. 5
Rand Leopold Desk Company 5
Recreation 90, 102
Development and 94
National Forests and 66–68
Redington, Paul 110
Religion 175
*Remedy for Disappearing Game Fishes, A* (Hoover) 112
*Report on a Game Survey of the North Central States* (Leopold) 111, 113
Riley Game Cooperative 115–116
Ringland, Arthur 39–40, 44, 45–47, 49, 50, 51, 58, 61, 62, 65–66, 71, 73–74
Rio Grande Valley (draining of) 54
*River of the Mother of God and Other Essays, The* (Leopold) 145, 181
Rocky Mountain National Park 20
Rogers, Keena. *See* Leopold, Keena Rogers
"Role of Wildlife in a Liberal Education, The" (Leopold) 145, 161
Roosevelt, Franklin Delano 120, 126–127, 137
Roosevelt, Theodore 12, 24, 31, 34, 42, 68, 74
*Round River* (Leopold) 157
Ryan, Christine 201

## S

*Sand County Almanac, A* (Leopold) xi–xii, 1, 15, 21, 31, 83, 123, 165–167, 168, 171, 175–176, 177–178, 181
Sangre de Cristo Mountains 47
Santa Fe, New Mexico 47, 49, 51, 52, 54, 56, 72, 134
Sargent, Charles Sprague 24
Save the Deer Club 164
Schmidt, Franklin 130, 136–137
Schottlaender, Alfred 136, 157
Schwartz, Charles 178
"Shack, the" 133–134, 137–141, 152, 153–156, 159–160, 171–173, 177, 178–179, 181, 182–183, 185–186, 201
Sitgreaves National Forest 89
Smith, Herbert 197
Soil conservation 87–88, 91–93, 119–120, 126, 145
Soil Erosion Service (SES) 126, 197
"Some Fundamentals of Conservation in the Southwest" (Leopold) 93
Sommers, Aldo 7

"Southwestern Game Fields" (Leopold) 93, 106, 110, 200
Sowls, Lyle 148
Spessart Forest 135
Sporting Arms and Ammunitions Manufacturers' Institute 107–108, 110–111, 115, 118
Spud (dog) 9
Starker, Arthur (uncle) 4, 189
Starker, Charles (grandfather) 1–4, 5, 7, 13–14, 14, 189, 190
Starker, Clara. *See* Leopold, Clara Starker
Starker, Marie Runge (grandmother) 1–2, 3–4, 4, 14, 189
Starker Lake 3
Starr's Cave 18
"Starvation Stalks the Deer" (film) 162
*State Journal* (Wisconsin) 162
Stinking Lake 72
Stoddard, Herbert L. 108, 110, 111, 137
Superior National Forest 90, 97, 201
Swift, Ernie 199

## T

"Thinking Like a Mountain" (Leopold) 167
Thompson, Dan 181
Thoreau, Henry David xii, 61, 167
Tic douloureux 171, 175–177
*Time* (magazine) 112
Tome Hunt Club 89
Trappers Lake 84, 90
Tres Piedras, New Mexico 49, 52, 56

## U

U.S. Biological Survey 108, 127, 128
U.S. Fish and Wildlife Service 61
United Nations 178
University of Wisconsin-Madison 103, 105, 107, 110, 129–131, 145, 147–152, 153, 178
  Arboretum 130–132, 145, 167–168, 172, 182, 197
  Department of Wildlife Management 156, 159, 165, 171
  Game Management Program 123–124, 150–152, 156

## V

Van Dyke, Henry 27
Van Hise, Charles 100
*Vegetable Mould and Earthworms* (Darwin) 31

## W

Wade, Doug 147
Walton, Izaak 98
"War Ecology" (Leopold) 161
Washington, D.C. 73
*Watershed Handbook* (Leopold) 93, 120
Waugh, Frank 95
"Wherefore Wildlife Ecology?" (Leopold) 147
White River National Forest 84
"Why a Wilderness Society?" (Leopold) 142
*Wild Life Conservation in Theory and Practice* (Hornaday) 72
Wilderness 16, 20, 84–86, 90–91, 94–96, 102, 141–143, 182, 201
Wilderness Society 132–133, 142
Wildlife 193
  Management 59, 110, 112, 137, 145. *See also* Game management
"Wildlife in American Culture" (Leopold) 161
Wildlife Refuges. *See* National Wildlife Refuge System
Wildlife Society, The 137, 142
Winchester Repeating Arms Company 71
Winn, Frederick 95
Wisconsin Academy 161
Wisconsin Alumni Research Foundation 152
Wisconsin Conservation Commission 161–163, 167, 178
Wisconsin Conservation Department 162, 199
Wisconsin Forestry and Conservation Department 105–106
Wisconsin River 133
Wisconsin's Scientific Areas 183
Wolves 163, 167. *See also* Predator control
World War I 77, 79–81
World War II 157–159, 168–169, 171
Writing process 150

## Y

Yale Forest School 24, 31, 33, 35–36, 37
  Pocono Mountain Camp 34
Yale University 31
  Sheffield Scientific School 31, 35
Yellow Thunder, Albert (Winnebago Chief) 131
Yellowstone National Park 20
YMCA 32
Yosemite National Park 102